Robert Poynton

Do Improvise

Less push. More pause. Better results.
A new approach to work (and life).

Published by
The Do Book Company 2013
Works in Progress Publishing Ltd
thedobook.co

This new edition published 2022

Text © Robert Poynton 2013, 2022
Illustrations © Nick Parker 2022

To find out more about our company,
books and authors, please visit
thedobook.co or follow us **@dobookco**

5 per cent of our proceeds from the sale
of this book is given to The DO Lectures
to help it achieve its aim of making
positive change: **thedolectures.com**

Cover designed by James Victore
Book designed and set by Ratiotype

Printed and bound by OZGraf Print
on Munken, an FSC-certified paper

A CIP catalogue record for this book
is available from the British Library

ISBN 978-1-914168-13-0

10 9 8 7 6 5 4 3 2 1

Contents

Let go notice more
use everything everything's
an offer use more
notice everything let go
LET GO notice go use more
everythings an OFFER LET
GO notice offers USE every
thing NOTICE GO LET everything
NOTICE MORE, use every offer
EVERYTHING'S an OFFER
nick parker 2022

Foreword

Skin in the game

When I wrote this book back in 2012, I knew some people would find it interesting and useful. I had a hunch that a few might become enthusiasts, even fans — and happily for me, I was right. But I never even dreamed that some would carve these ideas into their flesh. Yet they did. I know of more than one person who has the model at the heart of this book permanently inscribed, in ink, on their own body, as a tattoo. Talk about putting skin in the game.

Such commitment is touching for me and, as it turns out, well placed. As one enthusiast put it: 'The model is basically indestructible.' Over ten years later the central ideas have stood the test of time.

I haven't had any great revelations or a change of heart. I haven't had to invent a new language, or tinker with the model to fit changing circumstances. In a way, I have nothing new to say — nothing that changes the basics, anyway. The ideas still stand, as simple and obvious as they were when I first wrote about them. They are as relevant as ever.

This is striking. It is not as if nothing has happened in the last ten years. We are reminded of how unruly life is on a daily basis. Ideas and diseases spread at breakneck pace in unpredictable ways; technologies take off or disappear; markets soar or crash; a single act turns yesterday's hero into today's villain; your cute little children metamorphose into irascible adolescents. Companies no longer change, they 'pivot' — a term that may well seem quaint itself by the time you read this: the language itself changes, reflecting and amplifying all the other changes.

This is not exceptional. It is normal. It is the way things are. Over the last ten years, something that has always been true has become yet more obvious — namely, how little is under our control, at every level of scale, from the intimate realms of our social and professional lives, all the way up to the global society and planetary ecosystems we are inextricably woven into. We do not determine the flow of events.

Old ideas

This is an old truth. As Heraclitus of Ephesus said, over two thousand years ago: 'No man can step into the same river twice, for it is not the same river and he's not the same man.' Yet many of us feel discombobulated by the constant flux, as if immersed in a river in full flood, 'not waving, but drowning'.

The ideas in this book won't stem that flood. They do not provide an answer, or pretend to. Indeed, they suggest that the search for definitive answers is at the root of the problem. What they provide instead is a way to learn to float and swim, to steer your way through turbulent waters, enjoying an increasing sense of skill and finesse as you do. To do 'what you can, where you are, with what you have' and to derive satisfaction, even joy and delight, from doing so.

They are not some feature of a management fad, or tied to a particular technology. They have more in common with ancient and lasting traditions, like stoicism or Zen Buddhism, than today's trending topic. They are designed to enable us to deal with the unruly, messy, everyday reality that we try to ignore, but all have to deal with. No wonder they haven't changed.

New stories

If there is nothing new to say, then why a new edition? Zen master Shunryu Suzuki once said to his students: 'Each of you is perfect the way you are ... and you can use a little improvement.'

Over the past few years, my experience has deepened, not altered. The more I practise, the more I learn, and the more opportunities to practise I find. The deeper the embrace, the more powerful the connections to everyday life.

I have seen other people take these ideas to heart and use them, at home and at work, in ways I could not have imagined. This edition includes some of their stories, woven in between the chapters, to add other voices and perspectives to my own. They include facilitators, an educator, an artist and a writer.

I don't mean to suggest you should copy these people, but I hope you will be inspired to explore what works for you. When you hear what others have done, it puts flesh on the bones, giving you some insight into what you might do with this body of knowledge.

Each interview illustrates some of the ideas from the chapter it follows. That said, it is noticeable that people integrate the practices into the whole of their lives, so that it is hard to say where one ends and another begins ...

which is a lesson in itself. My model of the improv practices, like all models, pulls apart things that are woven together. The stories show that it is all connected. I hope this will encourage you to start wherever you like.

The illustrations for this edition (which are new) are another example of improvisation in action. The idea of how to do them emerged, unintended, through conversation. They were created quickly and easily, in a way that was enjoyable for Nick (who drew them), using a process that was itself improvised. So as well as illustrating the book, they illustrate the benefits of working this way (you can read more about this on page 154).

As befits a 'Do' book there are plenty of suggestions of things you can do. The most explicit of these are the games I have included in the final chapter. Long descriptions can, ironically enough, be interpreted as a kind of script, so I have chosen not to give you too much detail. This enables me to include more games and you to fill the blanks as you please. There are an infinite number of ways to use the games, so don't worry about getting it 'right'. Allow yourself to add to them or combine them. I encourage you not just to play them, but to play around with them.

The joy of uncertainty

In the last ten years my own understanding of these ideas and their relevance has evolved. They have taken me further than I could have imagined.

Improvisation is normally regarded as a last resort. It is what you do when all else fails. It is often regarded as a sign of failure. When I wrote this book I wanted to challenge that view. I had recently completed the building of our house in Spain and the experience had taught me that if you want to make anything, even a house, you need both planning *and* the ability to adapt creatively, i.e. improvise.

I would now go further. Uncertainty is not just an obstacle we need to navigate in order to get a result. It is the source of much of what is joyful, fulfilling and rewarding in life. I think we have things the wrong way round: what we imagine will bring us joy, creates much of our pain. And vice versa.[*]

The basic premise of our modern world is that we need to get somewhere else. According to this dominant narrative, once we do, everything will be fine. We need to get the kids into the right kindergarten (or school, or university); or get a new job, or a few more clients, or publish a book, or start another project. A big one for many people is to get to a position of 'financial security' (whatever that might be).

Whatever it is we are seeking, it always lies just over the horizon. We tell ourselves (and each other) that we are nearly there. That with a little more effort/money/ dedication/technology (delete or add your own as appropriate) we will soon arrive. We just need the right tool, or system, or hack, or app. Or a few more resources. But once we tick everything off and get on top of things, all will be well. Then we can be happy.

This logic is fantastical. As if we could reach the pot of gold at the end of the rainbow, or had never heard the story of the Midas touch.

John Lennon was right when he sang, 'life is what happens while you are making other plans'. It doesn't happen somewhere else. It is what happens here, now.

---

[*] A hat tip to Margaret Heffernan is due here. Her talks and writing helped me understand my own thinking much better.

We forget, or ignore, that if we could plan our lives down to the last detail — that would be deathly. Surprise, delight, joy, a sense of agency and identity all depend upon there being uncertainty. Quite literally, we couldn't do without it.

In that context, improvisation isn't just a tool to get you through the tough times. It is a way to develop the capacity to lead a fuller life. It gives you practical resources that allow you not just to cope, but to revel in the glorious, nuanced, incomprehensible and inevitable complexity of life. To meet the messiness of your own life without foreboding, every moment of every day. To live where you are and enjoy what there is, not hanker after where you might be or what you had hoped for.

It is easy to lose sight of this. Not because we are stupid, or slow, but because the important lessons in life are those we need to learn over and over again. As yoga teacher Lucas Rockwood says, 'Practise is everything.'

The path is made by walking

When I first wrote this book, my sons were children. They are young adults now. When I was their age, everything seemed simpler. You studied hard to get a good grade to get a good job. That was about it. There is simultaneously more ambiguity and more opportunity now.

As the Spanish poet Antonio Machado wrote: 'The path is made by walking.' The individuals of my sons' generation will have no choice but to make their own path. As a society, we need a new definition of what it means to live a good life. We will have to renew our systems and institutions before we know what new form they might take.

While it is undoubtedly true that we face multiple, interconnected crises, there is nothing special or temporary about this. Every generation likes to think they are unique. Fumbling around in the dark is the way of things.

Learning to live with that asks something different of us. Which is where I think the practices of improvisation make a contribution. Like scaffolding, they help us hold ourselves and shape what we are building, while we do so. No less important, they enable us to stay sane and enjoy each other's company along the way.

They are also simple and lasting, so if you like the look of them and want a handy reminder, you might even consider tattooing them onto your body.

1
The Promise

I was going to make chicken with olives. Cooking a traditional Spanish dish would, I felt, be a cunning way to show my new relations how well I was adapting to life in Madrid. But, as often happens, the dinner was postponed. Thursday suited me just as well as Tuesday, or so I thought. However, when I took the ingredients out of the fridge, a pungent smell declared that the chicken was no longer quite the thing to offer to guests.

So I had to improvise.

Into the bin went the chicken, along with my original idea and hopes of looking impressive. Instead I lashed up a boringly simple pasta sauce with onion, tuna and tomato. Yet my guests were impressed. My wife's Aunt Carmen asked what I had done to give it such a spicy tang. I was curious myself because I couldn't remember using anything spicy, so I shrugged it off, hoping to make it look as if there were a secret ingredient that was part of a master plan.

Unless buying the chicken three days too early counts, there was no master plan. However, there *had* been a secret ingredient. So secret not even I knew what it was. Only later did I remember that the previous night, my cast-iron frying pan had played host to some spicy little

Spanish peppers called 'pimientos de Padron'. It was the oil they had left behind that had given unexpected verve to my pasta sauce.

A complex world demands an improvised response

Cooking is frequently like this. As is life, and work. The unexpected is our constant companion. Blind alleys, unheralded turns and serendipitous connections are everyday stuff. Life is messy. However hard we work to avoid it, we are constantly accosted by things we didn't plan for, expect or want; from a puncture to a deflating economy.

This is not an exception, or a side effect. It is not our failing. It is the way things are. Life is a giddy torrent for which nobody has a script. Which, as we shall see, is actually just as well.

A complex world demands an improvised response. Even in theory, there could never be a script — all the money or computing power in the world could never produce one. The world, even our little bit of it, changes faster than we can track. Since everything is interconnected, it is unpredictable, and always will be. Our attempts to break it down into manageable pieces are of limited use, because wholes — like families, organisations or people — have properties that don't lie in the parts. Nothing stays still for long and everything falls apart. If a system is not responsive, it will fail. This is true for ourselves, our organisations and our society as a whole.

Yet somehow we cope. Prosper even. We succeed in ways we can't imagine and get results we don't expect, for reasons we couldn't anticipate. Though we rarely tell the story like that afterwards. Looking back, we draw straight lines between cause and effect, rationalising actions and decisions that were oblique or opaque at the time. We smooth things out, ignoring the fact that the struggle is where both the challenge and the joy lie.

We get by because we are naturally good at creative adaptation and there is a substantial measure of it in all that we do. So good, in fact, that we rarely notice it. We flex, respond, adjust, readjust, amend, refine, tailor or tweak what we are doing all the time. In short, like all living things, we are amazing improvisers.

Nonetheless, we generally ignore or disparage improvisation. Much of the time, we simply aren't aware of it. For example, on the first day of 'The Everyday Improviser', an online course I run with Gary Hirsch, one of the participants said:

> *If you had asked me an hour ago whether*
> *I improvised, I would have said 'no', but now*
> *I realise that every conversation is improvised*
> *because you are playing off what someone just*
> *said or something they have just done, so all of*
> *a sudden this is part of me, part of life.*

It was there all along, he just didn't see it. Not because it is mysterious, but because it is so ordinary. Improvisation isn't a special or peculiar skill that is the preserve of a talented few in the theatre. It is the ability to create a fitting response to events, as they arise, without relying solely on prior information or plans. In that sense, we are all improvisers. Every day, at home and at work, our lives are woven from the ebb and flow of complex loops of responses to responses to responses.

This is true at every level of scale, from our most intimate conversations to events on a world stage. The latter may play out at a slower rhythm, and it may be taboo to acknowledge it, but no one is in control, and our ability to predict events with any kind of confidence is far more limited than our leaders, or any of us for that matter, care to acknowledge.

In our culture, instead of being celebrated, improvisation is seen as a last resort, or a sign of failure. It is not respectable, particularly for people in positions of power or eminence, to improvise. When we catch them at it, we say, with scorn, that they are 'winging it'. For example, as film-maker David Keating says: 'In our industry "improvisation" is a dirty word. But plans alone won't make a movie, let alone a good one.'

This is a shame and a waste. By maligning improvisation we lose out on several counts.

First, we misunderstand our success. By ignoring how our amazing ability to improvise contributes to our achievements, we waste time and effort. We work harder and harder at planning and analysis, which are useful up to a point, but have diminishing returns. We push harder, doing more of the same, which makes us frustrated and stressed. Like a gerbil on a wheel, we end up running ever faster and going nowhere. This is exhausting, even damaging.

Secondly, we don't prepare ourselves as well as we could. If we only pay attention to the plan, we don't notice what else is going on. Which means we make (or repeat) mistakes we could avoid. There are more practical and economical ways to prepare for the messy realities we face (as we will see).

This also means that we don't develop our improvisational ability any further. We put a ceiling on a capacity that is more important than we realise, and could give us more than we imagine. We don't practise or grow the natural gifts we have. We use them more clumsily than we might.

By ignoring improvisation we ignore a part of ourselves, misreading our own nature. A great gift becomes an orphaned child that we banish from sight. As a consequence, something beautiful is lost. We act as if control and certainty would make us happy when, in fact, nothing could be further from the truth.

Margaret Heffernan, Professor of Practice at the University of Bath, is outspoken about the value of uncertainty. She says: 'Uncertainty is an absolutely ineradicable aspect of life — and it gets a bad press.'

She suggests a thought experiment to illustrate. Imagine you could know everything that was ever going to happen to you: who you will meet (and what they would say); how your career (or your marriage) will pan out; when, where and how you will die; even details like what you have for lunch each day. If so, then life would amount to 'waiting for the train'. It wouldn't be much of a life at all. If everything was scripted, it would not be a recognisable experience of being human.

Most of what we love in life — surprise and delight; the sense that what we do makes a difference; the feeling we have a choice; our ability to create things; our sense of identity — depends upon uncertainty. Which is why the ideas that improvisation rests upon hold such promise. They give us ways to understand how to nourish ourselves and guide our action so that we can live more deliberately and happily in 'the fertile void', instead of desperately trying to escape it.

The 'offer' here, as an improviser would say, is to learn to understand, trust and develop our ability to improvise. To become both more willing and more adept at flexing, adapting and adjusting to what we have, rather than wishing we had something else. This is more than a coping mechanism. It is what life is.

This takes no special talent or intelligence. It doesn't require any technology or a whole lot of theory. What it does take is curiosity and a willingness to make yourself available. If you cultivate that, your life can become easier and simpler, with more fun and less stress. You discover a way to get more out of life that doesn't rely on trying harder. To put it more prosaically, you can get more done, more easily. This is quite a prospect.

It is like learning a second language. Becoming fluent in another language enlarges your understanding. You see and hear things that you didn't see or hear before. You can connect with new people in a different way. It enriches how you think. A wealth of possibilities that were closed to you open up.

The promise of becoming a more fluent improviser is similar. It gives you a new dimension. Where before there were only problems, now you see 'offers' as well. Instead of lamenting setbacks, you focus on finding a way to use them. When you get stuck, you aren't fazed. You learn to pause because you know that paying close attention is a more fruitful response than madly rushing around. Difficulty doesn't disappear, but you engage with it, instead of struggling against it.

The TV series *Band of Brothers* tells the story of 'Easy Company' (of the 506th Parachute Infantry Regiment) in the Second World War. At one point they are about to enter a battlefield where they will be surrounded. Warned of this by a retreating officer, their commander replies: 'We're paratroopers, Lieutenant. We're supposed to be surrounded.'

Improvisers are supposed to be in the midst of turbulence. Volatile, uncertain, complex and ambiguous circumstances are their natural habitat. They seek uncertainty out because they know it is a source of novelty, possibility, joy and delight as well as difficulty and challenge. They relish and thrive in it.

They incorporate interruptions, objections and curveballs

seamlessly as they go. They are able, constantly, to build ideas and relationships, even in demanding circumstances. They show us that in order to shape and craft the stories you are part of, you don't need to control every element, all you need is a hand on the tiller. Happily, for the rest of us, they offer us some clues about how we can do that too, wherever we are in our life.

This means more than polishing a few neglected skills. It represents quite a shift in mindset. Instead of trying to bend events (and people) to your will, you focus on discovering a way to work with whatever you find. This can be very liberating. You realise that you don't have to know everything. That you don't always have to be 'on top of things', that you can allow yourself to be 'in the thick' of them. That you can use physical cues like position or space to cut through clever talk and create real action. A simple shift from 'yes, but' to 'yes, and' can make you a joy to work with and far more creative.

There are, in fact, plenty of sensible, intelligent and practical ways of behaving, many of which you already do, that don't require command or control. At its heart, this attitude is founded on humility and acceptance, which helps you to become more compassionate, especially to yourself. It is a lighter way of being.

Improvisational ability isn't a special talent you are born with but something we all have in some measure that can be practised and developed. Improvisers still prepare, but they prepare a territory, not a path. The aim of this book is to give you some ideas about how to do that and show you why it is worth the effort. Improvising well enables you to use the resources you have in a more satisfying, surprising and enjoyable way. A little can go a long way here. Simply accepting that life is messy and exploring how you might work with that can be a liberation.

Learning this new 'language' does not imply abandoning the old one, any more than learning Chinese implies forgetting your English. The aim is not to have one supplant the other but to broaden your repertoire and give you a new resource to work with. It is a complementary approach, not an alternative one. As an improviser would put it, it is a 'Yes, and ...' Of which more later.

People think of improvisation as unruly and chaotic but, in fact, it is a discipline with its own structure. This discipline has a number of uncommon virtues. It assumes that events around you, and the people that provoke many of those events, are beyond your control. As a result, it discourages you from wasting any time or energy trying, in vain, to control them. Instead, it focuses on how to use whatever they give you, even if it is a challenge or an objection, and trains you to see these as opportunities. It pays attention to what you can control, which is your own attitude and response to whatever happens. This seems very wise to me. Ultimately, the primary struggle that each of us face in life is with ourselves anyway.

A question of practice

The essence of the method can be captured in a small number of practices that you can understand quickly, remember easily and use forever. By practices I mean simple habits and questions that act as guiding ideas in any situation, and shape (but do not dictate) your response.

Thus improvisation is not at odds with structure: quite the opposite, it relies upon it. But it is a structure of a particular kind, which is generative, not constraining. I can explain how the practices work, but you are free to choose what you want to do with them.

The point is to do something. Reading about the ideas is one thing, but this is a book about doing, and the ideas explained here will only start to work for you once you put them into practice.

There are plenty of opportunities to plug the practices directly into everyday life. An infinite number, in fact. At any moment, when stuck, or floundering, or in search of something new or different, the practice of improvisation offers you simple questions that will provoke action (like 'how can I see this difficulty as something to use?'). It can be applied to almost anything. It won't give you a recipe, but it might help you cook up a different kind of life. The difficulty, if there is one, isn't finding opportunities to use the practice, but choosing amongst them.

To help with that, in the chapters that follow I have chosen to concentrate on three broad themes that are important to our organisations as well as ourselves, namely: communication, creativity and leadership.

Whatever you are interested in, improvisational practice offers you a way to act yourself into a new way of thinking (rather than think yourself into a new way of acting). By encouraging you to act differently, it creates the space for you to think differently. By engaging the whole person — body and soul — it short-circuits our cleverness and stops us thinking ourselves into a corner. It is light, not heavy or serious. It is also very simple. The main ideas can be explained in a single chapter, which is the one coming up. Take that on board and you can immediately set off on your very own inquiry.

The downside is that you need to be willing to be playful and have fun along the way. But that is just a price you have to pay.

Lisa Kay Solomon — *More options*

*Lisa Kay Solomon is a designer in residence and educator
at the Stanford d.school. Her focus is on helping others
to design the future. She is the author of several books,
including* Moments of Impact.

I first came across improv at Stanford University. It was the
most playful, engaging, expansive, growth-minded learning
I had done in such a long time. I was mesmerised. I left there
so alive. I had this feeling of: 'I don't know what just happened,
but I know I want to do this work more.'

At the heart of my work is design and facilitation. I want
people to be at the centre, not my programme, because
otherwise it is one way — a lecture, not a real learning
experience. So how do I design conditions to allow people to
grow, explore new ideas, and build connections with others?
How do I facilitate that in the moment? For both of these,
the ability to improvise is critical.

What gives me great hope is that these practices are
teachable and learnable. I start every class with some type
of collaborative, energetic, experiential activity. Every class.
We don't necessarily say it's improv because people shut
down, they might think, 'Oh no, I'm not an actor, so that's not
for me.' Instead, we say, 'We're going to warm up, we're going
to get present, be here.'

I think it should be mandatory for every single student
everywhere. We have a lot of rework to do, to thread this
into people's lives sooner. We used this approach with my
daughter's graduating high school class. We told them that
this is a playful way to build on all the deep, rigorous learning
you have done and bring it into the next chapter of your life,
which won't be as prescriptive as the first 12 years of your
education. Everything you have learned on getting an 'A' and

performing on tests is wrong now, it's not going to be primary any more.

Every time I design any meeting, even if the stakes are high, I am thoughtful about the first few minutes because that frames everything. If you can figure out how to get people to show up, let their shoulders down, lean in, listen and be in concert with someone else, then that's everything, isn't it?

Improv is also a strategy of resilience. When you're comfortable with improv, you realise you're never without options, which is the most extraordinary gift you can give someone. In today's age, filled with all this volatility and uncertainty, wouldn't you like never to be without options, even when your political system is falling apart, or there's a global pandemic? Wouldn't you like to feel you are able to make choices and see combinations that others aren't able to to even see?

But we don't frame improv this way, do we? We frame it as a craft thing that certain kinds of actors do, and you only study it if you are doing drama. The more that we think about improv as a practice for uncertainty and ambiguity, as a way to be a collaborative, generative partner, the better it is for society.

For me, to let go is a gift. For example, I think about how I want a meeting to go, but it may not go that way. Plans are just a starting point. My job is to be available for what happens in the room, not to strong-arm it to fit my intention. This allows me to notice differently. Do we have the right conversation happening? Do we have diverse inputs? Is this going too far one way? Do I need to slow it down?

If you come out of a great meeting, ask yourself, why did it go well, what happened, who was navigating well? Did they go at it, accept, block, dance together? We can become more attuned observers of excellence in action and notice the choice points that somebody had.

The other thing you can do is find a safe space to play a game. Maybe with your family, on a car ride, time-box it for five or ten minutes and try it out. If you put a little scaffolding behind it, you can hold it lightly. This isn't about getting it right, just see what happens.

What I am trying to do in my everyday practice is to help others feel they can make a different choice. These practices show that even within a disruptive context, you have some choice. This has helped me be a better professional and a better human — in my friendships and with my family. It has enabled me to have a little more grace, to honour people's fundamental humanity and what they need, which allows them to feel like their best selves.

—

lisakaysolomon.com

2
The Practice

**The practices of improvisation are very obvious. There is
nothing unique or special about them. This is not, as the
saying goes, rocket science. It is more like making a paper
aeroplane — with a little instruction everyone can do it.
You can then have endless fun experimenting with your
own variations.**

This may disappoint you — complex solutions can be
seductive. But once you get over your disappointment,
I am sure it will be a relief to realise that you won't have
to grapple with pages of equations, just make a few folds
in a sheet of paper, as it were.

These improv practices are not new. Indeed, they may
feel familiar. But originality isn't everything. Most 'new'
ideas are combinations of old ones anyway.

The ideas you will find here are simple as well as obvious.
They can be understood quickly and easily. There is subtlety
here, but the essentials can be covered in a single chapter.
Give me 20 minutes and you will be out of here, armed
with something you can use for the rest of your life.

This is a bold claim, but one I am happy to make, because
I know it is true. I am still learning from these ideas myself.
The interviews in this book are with people who have been

using them for years, if not decades. Workshop participants get in touch long after I met them, to say how it changed their life, or work, or relationships. This may seem remarkable, but it happens quite often.

One of the most beautiful things about working with these ideas is to see how a seemingly small shift can make such a big difference — one that lasts. Simple and obvious it may be. Trivial it isn't.

The practice can be summed up in six words. They are:

Notice More. Let Go. Use Everything.

You see, I told you we could do this quickly. Now that you have the basics you can start to use them. Let's try right here, right now, as you read this book.

How could you 'notice more'? Perhaps, as you read, you could observe the feelings that arise in response to my words. When are you curious, engaged, puzzled or frustrated? Notice that and you might learn something about yourself as well as about these ideas.

You could 'let go' of an expectation — that improvisation is frivolous, for example. That might help you see that you already do it, even if you don't have language for it, or pay attention to it.

You might 'use everything' by trying to explain one of the ideas to someone else (an idea you are struggling with perhaps?). Doing so will clarify what you understand and what you don't. Moreover, there is a good chance that the other person will give you a different way of looking at it. Even if they don't, by showing you value their opinion, you have given them a little gift. You have used your struggle to build a relationship. Nice move.

This goes on forever. With presence of mind, you can apply these ideas at any moment, in any context. You will always have new opportunities to notice more, let go and use whatever is available. At home, at work and at play. As often as you like, with whoever you like. It is a promiscuous practice.

Nonetheless, it acts as a discipline.

You don't need to keep learning new things, just practise familiar ones, which turn out to be endlessly useful. You can keep asking the same questions — the circumstances will bring plenty of novelty. This is economical. With practise, things become easier and, as golfers say, the more you practise the luckier you get.

It isn't a linear model. Each of the practices invites you to think about the others. Which means it doesn't matter where you start. Nick Parker, the illustrator of this book, explains how this works for him. He says:

> *In workshops, I will often find myself talking about my experience as it arises. For example, I might say something like: 'I **notice** that I am getting stuck on this. Is anyone else?' So I **use** my noticing to inquire into what is happening and **let go** of the idea that it is up to me to say something clever or funny.*

That's all of the practice, right there.

Remembering six words won't test your memory too much. But I can make it shorter. There is a single, three-word expression that we can hang the whole thing on. I call it the 'keystone' practice.

It is: 'Everything's an offer.'

This lies in the sweet spot. It sits at the intersection of 'Notice More', 'Let Go' and 'Use Everything'. To see everything as an 'offer' is to regard anything that happens as something you can use one way or another, which means paying attention and letting go of expectations that might limit how you use it. All three ideas are packed in. They come together as a coherent body of knowledge, which, just like a physical body, has distinct parts that hang together as a unit.

This not only saves us a whole three words but makes the practice ripe for summing up with a 'TLA' (three-letter acronym). Namely, EAO. Now we're down to three letters.

However, before we get too excited about this we should bear in mind Einstein's observation that 'everything should be as simple as it can be, but no simpler'. So, let's have a look at each of these ideas in a little more detail. There is nothing wrong with taking things to pieces as long as you remember that they are also connected.

Notice more

Normally, we don't notice very much. Certainly not in relation to the amount of information that is bombarding us, every second of every day (and I don't just mean social media posts, but the physical stimuli we are subject to all day long).

Our senses are not like scientific instruments, passively gathering information; they play an active role in screening much of it out. For example, the cells in the retina of the eye are arranged so that some signals are passed on while others are ignored. What we *perceive* is different from what we *receive*.

Much of this selection is automatic. It happens unconsciously and effortlessly. We are primed to give our full attention to things like food, fast-approaching cars and crying children, but most things tend to gently fade into the background, particularly if they aren't changing much. Happily, your conscious choices make a difference. You can choose what you pay attention to. And what you pay attention to becomes your life.

So, a good place to start is to notice what there is to notice. I would suggest concentrating on four broad categories: the wider world, the immediate environment, other people and yourself. That should just about cover it.

Try to 'lean into your senses'. Often we get wrapped up with what is going on inside our heads and don't really look, or listen. The mind always likes to have something to worry about. Imagination creates anxieties as easily as ideas.

Gary Hirsch does this by copying his dog, Luna. On a walk, she is completely immersed in sensing, which for her is mostly smelling. Inspired by her, Gary will try to do the same, leaning into his own senses. He will lavish attention on what he is seeing and hearing—the sound of birdsong, the pattern of scratches on a parked car and, yes, even the smell of cut grass in the park. This focus on sensation interrupts the loops of anxious thoughts he easily gets stuck in and, as he puts it, 'brings me home to myself'. The practice of noticing more can be very calming.

The challenge here is to get out of your head (as it were). Look at something as if you were trying to draw it. If it's a rose or a Ferrari, you may assume it is red without really looking. Is it really? Or do parts of it, from the angle you look, appear nearer black? Is it the same red all over? Focus on the sensation, not the label.

If a colleague (or partner) launches into a familiar speech, do you leap ahead and start to think of what you want to say next? Can you slow down, and listen to the words they actually say, not the ones you're expecting?

Can you listen for the intonation, for the pauses, for what they are *not* saying, for where the emotion lies, for how the rhythm varies? Can you listen to them as if you were going to repeat every word they said?

Or you could think about opening up, rather than leaning into, your senses. Can you include things that are on the edge? Can you learn to love the corner of your eye? Sit at your desk and listen. Can you let different things in, instead of filtering stuff out? Can you hear the air conditioning, the clock, the hubbub of voices, the photocopier, an aeroplane overhead, and still hear your own breathing? Can you take this kind of listening into a conversation? Can you stretch your listening to include people you don't normally notice? Can you hear new, different or dissenting voices?

Adam Morgan, founder of brand consultancy eatbigfish, argues that successful challenger brands do exactly this. They look outside the category they are in to find ideas and inspiration in areas that their competitors don't even notice. They might be in insurance but they look at what is happening in the world of coffee or underwear and use what they notice to build their business.

Another way to notice more is to make sure you are using all of your senses. We are primarily visual, so sight can easily dominate. Play around with that. If you want to listen better, try closing your eyes. You might not dare to do that in a meeting, but practise while you are listening to music and you can develop the ability to listen more deeply even with your eyes open.

Make sure you aren't abandoning whole senses. In the countryside, scent announces the opening of flowers, the onset of rain, the ripening of fruit, the proximity of water. Exhaust fumes and fast food aren't quite so attractive, so in a city we tend to close down our sense of smell altogether. Reactivate it. You might want to start in a coffee shop or a bakery, where the sensation is going to be more pleasant, but see if you can develop a willingness to notice the way things smell and the ideas and emotions that are sparked off as a result.

Notice more about your own body. It is more than a means of transport. It houses your mind, which isn't simply located in your head (for example, neurotransmitters that affect how we think are secreted throughout the body, particularly in the gut). Neuroscientist Candace Pert used the word 'bodymind' instead of either 'body' or 'mind', to remind us how interwoven the two really are.

Instead of getting lost in your thoughts, notice your posture, your breathing. Where do you hold tension (the jaw? the neck?). A skilful reading of your own body will not only tell you when you are tense but, for example, when to speak up and when to sit back, or whether the person across from you needs reassurance or encouragement and so on. This gives you a whole new source of information that will help you make decisions or have ideas. Learning to notice your own feelings and sensations is a practice in itself. Just because they are *your* feelings, doesn't mean you automatically know what they are — you have to notice them. Becoming a good reader of your own inner state is a skill you can learn.

Given how much we have coming at us already (from technology and social media in particular) some people say that the last thing they want to do is to let any more in. Which I completely understand. If that's an issue, then it can help to rephrase this practice as 'notice something else'. You might see something in the background, not the foreground.

The practice is notice more, not notice *everything*. I am not suggesting you should consume yet more 'content'. The idea is to pay attention to how you pay attention;

to invite yourself to notice something you don't habitually notice; or have yet to pay attention to.

You can learn to become more conscious, active and discerning about what you notice. You can deepen your capacity to be present to the world and, most importantly, to the people around you. Do so and you will find new possibilities and connections you never expected. In a sense, awareness is all. We should use it wisely.

Let go

Letting go sounds dangerous. From childhood onwards we are told to hold on. Hold on to Mummy's hand, hold on while the train is moving, hold on to that job. The idea that we should jettison or abandon things goes against the grain. What, then, does it mean, to 'let go'? What is it we need to loosen our hold on, and why?

There are lots of candidates. Can you let go of what you want to say next so that you can listen to what someone is actually saying now? It can be helpful to let go of micro-agendas, judgements, assumptions, beliefs, inferences, even aspects of your own (or someone else's) identity. But it is important to understand that this practice doesn't imply you should let go of everything, all at once. That would be stupid.

We need to let go of baggage from the past and extrapolations into the future, because they stop us paying proper attention to the present. And the present is where we live.

I see this very clearly in workshops. People can be quick to judge that what we are going to do is silly, or decide that they won't be able to do it. They arrive at a conclusion immediately. The same happens in everyday life.

We instantly conclude that John is dull or that his idea is a bad one without pausing to even take it in. This tendency is exacerbated by the 'Like' button. Technology encourages us to rate everything immediately in a simplistic way.

This makes life perversely difficult. If you instantly decide how things are, you give them no chance to become anything else. You allow yourself no room for manoeuvre and few options, which makes you tense or nervous. Your chances of responding in a way that is fitting or fresh are remote.

If you are going to work with what comes at you, and connect to the people around you, you have to be willing to let go of your expectations, because they won't have the same expectations as you. Without letting go, there is no space for anyone else.

This can be hard to see, not just because such snap judgements come so readily, but because they tend to be self-fulfilling, especially when it comes to judging ourselves. 'You see,' someone will say to me after a game, 'I told you I couldn't do this.' But they have made the experience fit their interpretation, not the other way round. At the cost of their own performance, they have made themselves right — and we do so enjoy being right.

This doesn't mean forgetting everything you know. Past experience is important, but it can stifle us. In this respect, your mind is a bit like your basement. Stuff has a natural tendency to pile up. If you don't keep clearing it out, it gets clogged up. You don't have to trash the lot but if you don't keep letting stuff go, it soon piles up again.

The other place our minds escape to is the future. We are as quick to generate expectations as we are to leap to conclusions. In some ways this is very helpful, because it enables us to act even when we don't have much information. However, it can also trip us up. If you are anything like me, your mind will always be on the lookout for something to worry about.

For example, when writing *Do Pause*, I got completely stuck on one particular chapter. The deadline was looming. My mind provided constant, critical commentary about what would happen if I didn't meet it, making me tense and stressed, and progress even less likely. The whole thing felt like a house of cards, on the brink of collapse.

In the midst of this I had a call with Kirsten Gunnerud (see page 68). She reminded me that the deadline was of my own making and suggested I let go of it. I resisted, spewing out all kinds of spurious reasons why I couldn't do that.

She tried another tack and invited me to take a pause (how ironic was that!). Still, I resisted. But she persevered and after about ten minutes I finally saw the sense of it and started laughing at myself. I gave up on the idea of working through the weekend, and when I came back to it refreshed on Monday, things clicked into place.

I was worrying about a future that had yet to happen. It was a story I had created for myself (which was perhaps why I clung so tightly to it?). And it paralysed me. It took someone else to jolt me out of it, which is a good point to note — sometimes you need other people to remind you of the practice. Many of the burdens we carry are of our own making. The practice of letting go is one way to put some of those burdens down.

This habit, of getting ahead of ourselves, shows up in many ways. You probably all know someone who will finish your sentences (perhaps you have *been* that person?). Improvisers have a term that is useful here: 'shadow story'. A shadow story is the expectation of how something is going to unfold. The person who completes your sentences is imposing their 'shadow story'. This prevents you from saying what you want to say. The flow of the conversation and the relationship both suffer as a result.

So 'shadow stories' are another good candidate to notice and let go of. As Gary says: 'There is such a quick leap from seeing someone come late to the meeting, to deciding they are a bad person.'

You can't stop shadow stories forming, so you have to recognise them for what they are and let them go. As soon as you let go of one, another will come along just behind it, so there is plenty of opportunity to practise. Don't try to stop them coming along; all you have to do is open up a little space for the present moment by letting them go. That can make all the difference.

Use everything

If everything is an offer, there must be plenty of offers out there. Indeed, there are. An infinite number, in fact.

The all-encompassing nature of this idea is one of its strengths. It deliberately supposes that whatever you face, regardless of how inviting or irksome it may seem, is usable in some way. Whether you like it or not, expect it or not, wish for it or not, you should ask yourself how you can use whatever is happening to you, around you or within you. This denies you any wriggle room and forces you to look harder, which is the point. This is what makes it a rigorous and disciplined practice.

Nonetheless, it is useful to acknowledge the variety of what is available. Otherwise you might ignore or dismiss categories that turn out to have very rich pickings.

Let's start with you.

You may be glad to know that all your errors and mistakes qualify as offers. This is an incredibly powerful and positive reframing.

If you see mistakes as offers, you learn fast. You may learn how *not* to do something, or use the experience to understand why something didn't work. You might also discover something you weren't looking for, which is how many of the most important discoveries get made (like penicillin, or the continent of America, for example). You can see a mistake as a 'mis-take', like an actor on a film set, and regard it as another take, or attempt, in an iterative process that strives to get better.

This doesn't mean you should make mistakes on purpose, but given that they are going to occur anyway, it provides a constructive way to respond and a good way to direct your energy. If mistakes are opportunities, you don't need to make apologies, look for scapegoats or find excuses: you just get on with working out how to use them.

Another group of potential offers is failures and breakdowns. If you have a glue that fails to stick permanently you might use it to invent the Post-It note. If the projector fails, use it as a chance to have a conversation. Or to create simple, hand-drawn visuals. Or to get people to talk to each other instead of listen to you.

Gary is great at this. He once lost his glasses on the way to a workshop and used it to create a sense of intimacy with the group he was working with — he had to get everyone really close so he could see them. During the Covid pandemic, when we all had to start working online, he found ways to use objects people had lying around the house to create new games and exercises. (Note that to do this he had to 'let go' of his own shadow story about working online, which he had previously dismissed as dull and limited.)

Misfortune, as well as mistakes, can also be regarded as offers. The second time I had Covid it lasted a month and I was exhausted all the time. It was January, when I think about what I want to do in the year to come. The sluggishness of my thought made it easier to get in touch with what I felt, and therefore what I really wanted. This didn't make having Covid any better, but it turned out to have its uses.

Other people are a constant source of offers. They bring interpretations, experience and perspective that you don't have. When I first organised a Reading Retreat I didn't know how to choose the books, so I asked the participants to suggest three each and bought those. This saved me work *and* got them engaged. Other people will provide all manner of fodder for your process, whether they mean to or not. Indeed, even the people who reject your ideas provide a raft of offers, though you might have to work a bit harder to see them.

There is an improv game where a storyteller is given words that have nothing to do with the story they are telling. The word-giver is invited to be as obstructive as possible. Nonetheless, despite the fact they are intended as obstacles, the storyteller ends up finding the words a help. This is because the game forces you to regard them as offers. (See 'Swedish Story' on page 151.)

You can apply the same rules at work or at home. If someone says 'no', you could see it as a request for more information. Or as a test for your ideas. Or you could look for a way to associate, include or connect their objection, which will change your idea, and strengthen it, maybe even improve it. If someone sees things differently from you, instead of thinking they are wrong, see it as an offer. Ask yourself how their point of view can enrich yours.

Can you see what isn't there? In a famous story, Sherlock Holmes brilliantly uses the fact that the dog *didn't* bark in the night to solve a crime. Ingvar Kamprad, founder of IKEA, once stood in a huge Chinese poultry market, surrounded by thousands of plucked chickens, and asked, 'What do they do with all the feathers?' He saw what wasn't there as an offer, which IKEA then used as a source of filling for bedding. Ask yourself what is missing or absent and see how you could use that too.

You don't need much to work with. When I started Yellow,* one of the first people I spoke to about participating winced when I mentioned his title (he was a CEO). It was only a fleeting gesture but it made me think. As a result, we asked people to introduce themselves without mentioning their title or job or industry. It seemed like a small detail at the time, yet it turns out to have been really important — it allows people to encounter each other as individuals, which creates a different kind of relationship.

Sometimes you don't have much anyway, and you can use shortages to spur your ingenuity. When Robert Rodriguez made the film *El Mariachi*, he didn't have any proper lighting. He used that to make the movie 'moody'. He set it in a small town in Mexico and made a guitar case central to the story, because that was all he had. If you want to use what you have, an obvious and easy place to start is simply to ask yourself, 'What have I got?' You might be surprised at how much you have overlooked (it also reconnects you to the practice of noticing, as you have to pay attention to what you have).

If 'use everything' feels overwhelming, try 'use anything' or 'anything and everything can be useful' instead. If it frees you up, rephrase it to suit yourself.

Unforeseen consequences, accidents, acts of God, disasters and delays can all be used to your advantage, if you are prepared to consider them as offers. I have

---

* Yellow is the venture I started in the 2020 pandemic with Alex Carabi. It comprises small, online learning groups that meet for two hours every two weeks for five months. For more information: yellowlearning.org

colleagues who have found value in getting on the wrong plane or having their car crushed during a workshop. That doesn't make these good things. But it does stop you thinking of them as bad things. In other words, thinking in terms of using everything reminds you to let go of judgement. You see, it all fits.

An infinite game

I began by saying that the practice is simple. But that doesn't make it easy. Simple and easy are not the same thing at all. The rules of chess are simple enough to be explained in a few minutes — but chess isn't easy.

The first thing to notice is that it isn't enough to know about these ideas, you have to *do* something with them. That is why they are called practices.

There is no goal or end point. This kind of practice isn't a task you can complete. It won't give you an answer, but a stream of options. Which is a relief. You can be gentle on yourself, try things out and see what happens, in your own way, in your own good time. There are an infinite number of opportunities to practise, so it doesn't matter that you will miss some (most of them, in fact). Nor is there any shame in forgetting to practise, because you can come back to it at any moment (something I frequently find myself having to do).

Your practice can be patient and reflective. These ideas have emerged from improv theatre but that doesn't mean they are only useful for the immediate or spontaneous response. You can mull over where there might be an offer, or what else you might notice, or what you can let go of, for as long as you need to.

Since you can start anywhere, you might want to build on strength and begin with the practice that comes most readily to you (most people have a preference). Or you could do the opposite, and choose to work with that you find most difficult — which might be where you have most to gain. For example, if (like Kirsten Gunnerud — see page 68) you are using the practice with kids you might find that noticing more comes quite naturally, so letting go might be more useful to them.

The more you do, the more you learn. The more you practice, the easier it becomes. But to get going, you have to be willing to be changed, which might require some letting go. This is because improvisational practice challenges habits and beliefs that are woven so deeply into the fabric of our thought that we don't notice them.

For example, we think we can explain someone by analysing their answers to a standardised questionnaire and putting a label on them. We try to compose high-performing teams by putting the right 'components' together, as if people were parts of a machine. We demand strategies that are 'future proof' when we have little idea what the future holds. We set 'deliverables' for a creativity course. We give scientists research grants, but only if they can tell us, in advance, what they will discover.

The invisibility of such assumptions means that ways of thinking which challenge them just seem plain wrong. Our education is lopsided. Years of formal and informal schooling would have us believe that the certain, rational, objective knowledge is the only kind.

Improvisational practice challenges this view. For example, it says that you don't deal with something complex by trying to break it down into pieces. It suggests that our enthusiasm for measurement, analysis and prediction is misguided, and that these activities are often pointless or counterproductive. It suggests that always trying to control what happens is not possible, necessary or even desirable.

The practice asks something different of you.
It encourages you to engage as a whole person (not just a rational mind) in an intuitive way. It welcomes all of you to the game. It recognises and values information that is gathered via feel, bodily sensation, posture and movement. It generates 'sensuous knowledge' not book learning. It values speed, responsiveness and fit over accuracy, precision or regularity. It gives precedence to creating a flow of ideas and energy rather than arriving at answers. It is a living example of the scientific insight that very simple behaviour (or rules) can quickly generate creative complexity.

It selects ideas and actions through evolution rather than evaluation. It demonstrates that we can exert influence and impart direction without control. It emphasises practice over theory and action over conclusions.

Be aware, however, that it won't tell you what to do. As should be obvious by now, these ideas are general, universal even. They are more like a compass than a map. A compass shows you which way is north, but only you know which way you want to go, and you must observe the terrain for yourself.

This not only leaves room for you, but requires that you show up, which isn't as easy as it sounds. Especially when you find yourself questioning long-cherished but unconscious beliefs. Not once, but again and again.

I think you will find it is worth it. Just as this way of working can generate seemingly magical stories on stage, it can help each of us, individually and collectively, live more rewarding and creative lives, and create more valuable and sustainable organisations.

If you want to know how, read on.

Nick Parker — *Mantras*

*Nick is a writer who also draws. Much of his work is on
tone of voice. He has written books on reading, toast and
a volume of tiny stories entitled* The Exploding Boy.
He is also the illustrator of this book (see page 154).

Reading *Do Improvise* was brilliant for me, because it gave
me a way to express things that had been instinctive and
half formed. It codified a few simple ideas into a kind of
mantra that I could use for myself, or with others.

When we craft an elegant phrase, it is like inventing a really
useful thing, for example, 'The Project Management Triangle',
which says that you can have any two of *fast–cheap–good*,
but not all three. Once you can say them to yourself, they
help you see the world differently. So I collect them.

'Let go, notice more, use everything,' is one of these.
I call it a mantra because it is literally chantable, I can (and
do) walk along saying to myself, 'notice more', 'let go' or
'everything's an offer, Nick'.

It has become so much a part of how I move through the
world that it is difficult to isolate it. But, for example, if I am
doing a job for a client, it is a way of reminding myself to
speak to the less obvious people, to be attentive, even in
a break in a workshop because, frankly, it's ridiculous how
often the 'penny-dropping' ideas will crop up in the little
offhand moments, not in the big exercises.

The unexpected and really fruitful shift for me was the
way these ideas affected me in my personal life, particularly
around the idea of 'notice more'. I was always good at
noticing more in the outside world, but I started to notice
that you can notice more about your internal dialogue,
your own thoughts and feelings, and then you can articulate
how you are feeling.

So, in conversation I can say, 'I notice this energises me,' or 'I notice I am quite unsettled by this idea.' That idea of being self-reflective, commenting on what is going on for me right now, is really helpful. It makes things less charged, less personal. It is different from saying, 'Your idea makes me uncomfortable.'

One tangible example of how it has affected me is when I broke my leg, which I did in a very stupid way, walking up the garden path in the dark. I remember straight away thinking, 'So this is where we are,' with no sense of annoyance or frustration.

Of course, I was in a lot of pain. But I also remember feeling, 'This is what I am doing now'; I am in a hospital, then at home, with my foot up, unable to move for six weeks.

People kept saying to me 'poor you', but I genuinely didn't feel sorry for myself. That wasn't because I was looking on the bright side, trying to make myself feel cheerful about something that was rubbish. It was because I was aware that this was just very different from what I had expected.

I asked myself what I could do with six weeks lying in bed. I am pretty sure that this indirectly came from years of using the mantra of 'everything's an offer'.

What I did was finish writing a book because that seemed like the offer. This is not just about putting on a brave face, it is about being genuinely open to what is really going on, rather than feel it was unfair, or blame myself.

For me, this isn't just about responding to something bad or unexpected, and it is more than a way of coping; it is a way of seeing and being in the world. If you are trying it out, my advice would be to *literally* use it as a mantra. Walk around saying it to yourself …

—

nickparker.co.uk

3
Communication

Communication is what you do all day. And improvisation is a big part of how you do it.

All day long you are constantly communicating with and responding to other people — in person, on the phone or online. Everything, from a chat in the café to a high-stakes negotiation, passing through emails, meetings, presentations and conference calls (video or otherwise) is communication. If you are any kind of leader or executive, communication is what you get paid for. It is what you do with your friends. It is what makes your marriage work (or not). It is how you bring up your kids.

Communication is a complex, social, improvisational dance. We are more than postmen, delivering sealed messages. We are the messages. We are constantly responding to others' responses. As we communicate, we exchange and relate not just factual information, but emotion and identity.

You constantly sense what is being said, on many levels. You adjust what you say and how you say it as a result, ceaselessly, and almost without thinking. However structured the conversation, most of the words you say are chosen spontaneously. And you speak with more than words.

You delicately vary tone, inflection, rhythm and volume in response to what others say. Depending on the medium you are using, you will also use gesture, position, posture and facial expression. You take into account timing, sequence, atmosphere, media and setting.

When we communicate well it is a great source of satisfaction, even joy. This highly intricate dance is a capacity we all show, in everyday life. In all sorts of contexts, it is through communication that we make sense of things, build ideas and create value. We feel connected and appreciated. Good communication is central to our effectiveness and our happiness.

Conversely, when we don't communicate well it is a source of frustration, confusion and anxiety. 'Bad communication' is the most common complaint in organisations, with few exceptions.

This isn't surprising. Human communication is incredibly complex and multi-layered. There is so much going on, and so much opportunity for misunderstanding, that, in a way, it is amazing that people ever communicate successfully at all. And yet we do — even online, where the subtleties are diminished and some kinds of information are missing entirely.

As social beings, we are naturally adept at communication. However, this gift is also a curse. Our communication is so instinctive that how we go about it becomes invisible. We can easily fall into unhelpful patterns or behaviours that are hard to see, let alone change.

X-ray meetings

This is where the improv practice comes into play.

It offers us a lens through which to look at what is going on when we communicate. It lays bare, in very simple terms, what is going on. It x-rays our conversation. For example, if you look at your meetings through the lens of the improv practices, irrespective of what they are about, you can see what is happening.

Are people listening to each other? Do they build on each other's contributions? Are they willing to be changed? Who is being obstructive or 'blocking'? (If it's you, why is that?) Asking any of these questions will help you understand why you have the kind of meetings you have (whether they are good, bad or indifferent) and do something about it. What improv does is provide a very simple set of ideas to help you frame what you are saying and doing.

You don't immediately have to change things. Sometimes, understanding them is enough. For example, Kathy left her job in a big company and began to work as a consultant with the company she had left. A former colleague now became her client. She quickly found herself feeling frustrated and confused. When she looked at the situation through the improv lens, she realised that the vast majority of her offers were being blocked. Seeing this helped. It enabled her to understand why she was feeling frustrated.

She also noticed that in her new role as a consultant, it was her job to be an 'offer launcher'. Many of her offers were bound to get blocked — that came with the territory. She needed to let go, not just of the job, but of her idea of her old role so that she could accept this new reality. She didn't need to change anything. The understanding that looking through the improv lens gave her was enough to make her feel very differently about the situation.

It is tempting to focus on the other guy, but it is important to apply this lens to our own communication. For example, if I feel John always says 'no' to my suggestions, I should scrutinise my own behaviour, not just blame him for being negative. What might I be doing (or not doing) that leads to him saying 'no'? Maybe he feels I am blocking him and is just responding in kind? This is very common. Few of us notice the blocks that we ourselves dish out.

Try this. Listen out for all the times you say 'yes, but ...' (or words to that effect) and try and turn them into 'yes, and ...' That will raise your awareness of how often you block without realising.

You might also ask yourself who you are really listening to — other people, or your own inner voices? Are you bringing baggage, 'a shadow story', from previous conversations into this one? Are you making clear offers? Do you use the offers people are giving you? Are you more concerned with how you come across or with what other people say? Asking such questions of yourself is a way to look at yourself through the eyes of other people, which, as we shall see, is absolutely fundamental to good communication.

When I introduced these ideas to my friend Adam Morgan he made an astute observation. He said: 'Improv shows you the basic building blocks of communication and relationships. It gives you a fundamental grammar.' Understanding the building blocks enables you to think about how you construct your communication. This includes more than the words you say.

Film director David Keating uses 'the ideas that improv rests upon' to inform his film-making. On a film set, pressure is high, time is short, people don't know each other well and there is a very hierarchical form of organisation. For his horror film *Wake Wood*, which was shot mostly on location in rural Ireland, David felt that it was very important that he, the director, was present for the whole crew. Literally.

He decided to arrive at the location very early every morning. He spent some time, alone, on the set thinking through the day's shooting, and by the time the crew arrived he would be visibly working at his trestle table. Every day, he would set up his stall precisely where the bus arrived, so that people could see him.

This action was a powerful piece of communication — part carrot, part stick. The carrot was to make himself accessible to everyone, so they could contribute their ideas and suggestions. Being 'in their faces' like this made it easier for anyone to talk to him. The stick was to show them that, unlike some directors, he, the leader, was physically present and committed. Implicit was the notion that everyone else better had be too.

Communication is connection

So far, I have focused on interpersonal communication. I have done so deliberately because, even with all the media we have at our disposal, everyday interaction is still the most widespread and all-pervading form of communication there is. Ignore it and you miss most of the action.

However, there is another important reason for this focus on the interpersonal. It shows us, very clearly, that communication is, at heart, all about connecting people. The word itself, which comes from the same root as 'communion', confirms this. It means to share.

It is my firm belief that all forms of communication are, or want to be, two-way. Communication is more than the transmission of data. For communication to happen, there must be an exchange of some kind — a stimulus and a response. Something goes out and something comes back as a result. What comes back may be of many different kinds — a speech might elicit cheers, boos, a witty riposte or a vehement counter-argument — but if it is only one-way traffic you have no communication.

Much of what is commonly called 'communication' in the political and marketing worlds is, in fact, anything but. It is only one-way. It would be more accurate to describe it as 'propaganda', but that doesn't sound very attractive, so it gets 'rebranded' as 'communication'. This sleight of hand confuses things.

At some level, communication, if it is to be worthy of the name, has to be about what happens between people. This is obviously true of personal communication, but it is also true of meetings, presentations, conferences and even mass communication.

For example, irrespective of their politics, great speakers like Winston Churchill or Martin Luther King make a personal connection with everyone listening. Whatever you think about his politics, Donald Trump is brilliant at this. Gifted communicators see and acknowledge their audience, so that they feel included, even if they can't literally talk back. Thus, even in a broadcast to millions, it feels like someone is talking to you.

The opposite is true as well. I once went to a Sting concert in a stunning, natural outdoor arena in the Sierra de Gredos. In stark contrast to the warm-up band, Sting and his musicians seemed oblivious to the surroundings and the audience. However technically accomplished a performance it may have been, I felt there was no communication and therefore no connection, which in my view made it a disappointing concert.

The failure to appreciate this intrinsically two-way nature of communication accounts for much of what people complain about. The single biggest issue is forgetting, ignoring or excluding the audience.

For improvisers, forgetting the audience is lethal, so they do all sorts of things to create the connection and keep it open and alive. You can use the same ideas to remain connected to your own audiences. Do so, and you will communicate much more effectively.

Let's look at presentations. Every day, millions of people agonise over their Powerpoint slides, fretting over the details of the content. Yet in every presentation there are three elements. You, your material and your audience. Of the three, the material is the one that matters least. Yet the vast majority of people focus almost exclusively on the slides. Hardly anyone ever thinks in a disciplined way about what the audience needs. So what can you do about this?

Consider the audience

The people in your audience have needs of their own that have nothing to do with your agenda. If those needs aren't met, they won't be able to listen to you. There is a kind of unspoken deal in play — if you don't attend to them, they won't listen to you.

This is a big point. Even when you are giving a presentation, communicating is as much about listening as it is about speaking. You might be the one doing most of the talking, but that doesn't mean you have licence to get wrapped up in yourself. You need to push your attention out to the people you are talking to. You serve yourself best by serving them.

This is partly about being sensitive to the room. My colleague Gary Hirsch and I once ran a workshop in

Thailand where we expected about 40 people. Only six turned up. Nonetheless, we spent the first five minutes behaving as if we were talking to a room full of people, because that is what we had prepared. It took us a while to realise that with only a handful of people, we could have a conversation with them.

Mis-reading the room like this is remarkably easy to do, so we coined a piece of language to stop us doing it again. We call this 'the whites of their eyes'. This is a reminder to consciously check what is needed, once we are in the room with the audience and can see 'the whites of their eyes'. This forces you to think about how you are going to make a connection with them and stops you drifting off into your own little world.

We fleshed this idea out to create a tool to help you meet your audience's needs. It consists of five simple questions, which you answer from the audience's perspective. They are:

1. Trust the driver — why should they listen to you?

2. Who are they listening to, beyond labels?

3. What is expected of them; what are they going to have to do?

4. What will they get as a result of listening?

5. Are they being seen and acknowledged?

You can apply these at any level of scale — for a big presentation, small meeting or even an individual conversation — though it really comes into its own with a sizeable audience.

1. Trust the driver

Trusting the driver is about credibility. The audience wants to know why you, in particular, are worth listening to. What experience or understanding or insight do you have that makes you credible on this subject? This doesn't mean you need to be (or pretend to be) an expert. It means you need to give them some reason to trust that you are worth listening to, rather than assuming that you have the right to command their attention.

For example, when using improv with a business audience, I will explain my background is in business not the arts. When talking to Spaniards, I might use some Spanish slang that demonstrates I know the country. If I am working with Nike, I will tell them I have worked with Nike before, and so on.

2. Who are you (the speaker) beyond labels?

If communication is about creating a connection between people, your audience needs to know something about who you are as a person, beyond labels. Not everything, but something. You may be Director of Operations, but *who* are you? This is mostly about small details, but those details make a big difference.

The need can often be met very quickly, through something as simple as body language — do you stride out, or amble on? The form of your name you choose is another option — are you 'Rob' or 'Robert Poynton, Associate Fellow of Green Templeton College, Oxford'. You might mention some unexpected personal detail, taste or interest. How you dress has an effect, so think about that in advance. This isn't about being confessional, it is about adding a humanising touch.

One great way to show who you are is to play with status. For example, a powerful CEO might play low status by mentioning how his kids were defying him that morning. Coming down from a high-status position is a particularly effective way to create a connection. You can do this, quite literally, by abandoning the podium. I will sometimes start a workshop sitting on the floor, which puts me below my audience, who are sitting on chairs, changing my relationship to them.

There are many different ways to do this. You could tell a story, or make an observation, or ask a question, but one way or another, to give the audience an idea of who you are, it has to be personal.

3. What is expected of the audience; what are they going to have to do?

This is one people normally don't think of. After all, it seems self-evident that the audience is there to listen. That may be true, but even if they are a captive audience, you shouldn't assume they are willing to listen. That is their choice.

In fact, there is normally something more you want an audience to do. You might want them to listen out for certain things; to answer some questions, or come up with questions for you; to give you feedback, or report back to someone else; to take part in an exercise, or participate in a reflective conversation afterwards. Whatever it is, let them know upfront. If you don't, they will be busy wondering what it is they are meant to be doing, instead of listening to you.

4. What is the audience going to get as a result of listening?

People always want to know what's in it for them. Quite right, too. If they are going to give you their time and attention, it makes sense that they want to know what they are going to get in return. So tell them. Are they going to get some new ideas? Or some tools? Or a chance to play?

Once again, the important thing here is to show that you have thought about it. Different people might, in reality, get quite different things from what you say, but what matters is showing that you have their interests in mind. This is different from trying to control how they respond.

Again, the possibilities are infinite. Bear in mind it isn't necessarily information you are giving them; it could be a new perspective or the chance to disconnect from other worries.

5. Is the audience being seen or acknowledged?

Even though the presenter is in the spotlight, the audience still needs to be seen. If you ignore this, it has consequences. When an audience hasn't been seen they will often disengage, or behave badly, in order to be seen. So communication breaks down.

When improvisers ask their audience to suggest an occupation, someone will often shout, 'Proctologist'. They don't really want to see a scene about a rectal examination, they want to be seen themselves. Which is part of the reason that improvisers ask for suggestions — it 'sees' the audience.

In a business setting, people will often raise awkward questions or objections if they don't feel seen. We will explore how you might deal with these in a moment, but it is important to realise that if you see the audience well in the first place, you will prevent many of these obstacles from occurring at all. This is particularly important if you want approval for a proposal of some kind. Make sure you acknowledge the audience early on, or they will make themselves seen by saying 'no' to whatever you are proposing.

With a presentation, this can be as simple as acknowledging that the room is half-empty, or packed to the gills, or that it is late. It doesn't necessarily have to be something the whole audience share. You can see a whole audience by picking out a detail and seeing one person, e.g. 'John told me as we were coming in that this has been a difficult week.' The rest of the audience will empathise.

This is exactly what is going on when a rock star at a stadium concert says, 'Good evening, Glastonbury!' If we are in the crowd, we feel great because we feel seen. This isn't logical — even the most drug-fried rock star really *ought* to know where he is — but even so, the crowd loves it. A connection is created.

You can even use the reluctance of an audience to participate as a way of seeing them. When a suggestion in a workshop gets no response at all, Adam Morgan will often say, 'I will take silence as a sign of enthusiastic assent,' using the audience's behaviour as an offer and seeing them in the process.

These questions serve as a check list. Write down what you are planning to do to meet each of these needs in the first few minutes (which is where you win over — or lose — your audience). It needn't be much; audience needs can be met very quickly, sometimes simultaneously.

This is very easy to do. I often forget until the last minute and find myself in the taxi on the way to a meeting hurriedly going through the questions. Even at this late stage, it still helps. I invariably find something I had missed and make changes as a result. Improv isn't always about being spontaneous. The emphasis it puts on the audience's needs, above your own, provides us with tools like this that can help you prepare.

Feel the fear

It is curious that we so easily forget to think about something as important as what the audience needs? Why is this? One reason is fear. We worry enormously about what other people think of us. So much so, that it is easier to look the other way. We invest the details (like bullet points or typefaces) with importance to avoid confronting the more difficult issues. Instead of focusing on what is important, we focus on what we can control, namely — the slides.

By contrast, improvisers understand that an audience, while scary, is also very supportive. They know that people do not like to watch failure, so at some level they want you to succeed.

This seems contradictory but I don't think it is. The stage itself is a useful metaphor. It is flat and supportive, but it has a sharp edge, not a gentle one. Step over this and you plummet into the orchestra pit. An audience is similar. If you take them into account, they will be supportive and forgiving. But fail to attend to their needs and they are ruthless. Their attention and engagement cuts off suddenly, just like the edge of the stage. Using these questions is a way to keep you away from that edge.

I don't mean to say that the role of content in a presentation is irrelevant. Good slides lift things and great material can, occasionally, carry the day. For example, there is a magnificent TED talk by statistician Hans Rosling (author of 'Factfulness') whose animated visualisation of data is stunning. But these animations were the result of decades of work. And, realising that there is more to presentations than good data, at the end, Rosling strips off to reveal a spandex vest and goes on to swallow a sword (or, to be more accurate, a 19th-century Swedish infantry bayonet). Really. Check it out.

Going off piste

I am often asked about how to field questions or objections. These are scary because the things people raise are beyond your control. But if you really want to communicate, offers from the audience, of any kind, are a godsend. An aggressive question can be a thumping big offer, if you are willing to treat it as such. Moreover, responding well to such curveballs is one of the quickest and most effective ways to connect with an audience.

The first thing is to let go of the idea that you need to know *everything*. Much of the anxiety comes from the feeling that you have to be able to answer any question definitively. This only inhibits you. Give it up. Allow yourself to *not* know. Some questions can't be answered, some objections don't deserve your attention, some things aren't appropriate to deal with in public and some things, however interesting, don't suit your purpose in the moment.

So you need to know what matters to you in the moment. You have to have a clear grasp of your purpose and how unfolding events serve or impede your progress towards it. A superficial understanding of improvisers suggests that they say 'yes' to everything, but that isn't true. They are constantly choosing which offers to accept and which to block based on what the story needs next. They will quite happily block offers that feel like blind alleys or distract from the main thrust of the story. They do so quickly and instinctively, and they develop a feel for the offers that feed their story. You can do the same.

I once ran a workshop for a disaster-response team in Asia. During one session I was asked how the cultural complexities around saying 'yes' or 'no' played out in different Asian cultures. I tried to answer it. This was a mistake. What was I thinking? I don't know anything about Asian cultures so my response was vague, unhelpful and made me look foolish. I had been seduced by my position. Being at the front of the room made me feel that I *ought* to answer. I would have done much better to follow Mark Twain's example: 'I was gratified to be able to answer promptly and I did. I said I didn't know'.

Twenty minutes later, I did exactly that. I was asked about how to react to the deception and deceit that can occur during disasters. Fresh from the earlier embarrassment, I answered with a block. I acknowledged I didn't have an answer and pointed out that it wasn't possible to address such a complex question in the middle of a workshop with 40 people. Heads nodded all around the room, including the head of the person who had posed the question (who at least felt seen, even if they didn't get an answer).

So blocking has a place. It is a legitimate response. If you let go of the idea that you have to answer everything immediately, it will help you deal with the anxiety that difficult questions can provoke.

Most of the time, however, you will want to create flow, so you won't want to block. No prizes for guessing this means noticing more, letting go and using everything. Listening is hardly a radical suggestion, but the trouble is that when faced with a question or objection, we often don't do it. The anxiety of being put on the spot can make the mind race, or go blank. It is all too easy to veer off into your own thoughts, or leap ahead to a prepared response, or answer a different question. Instead, make a conscious effort to listen to the actual question you are being asked, by this person, in this moment.

Your body is your friend (and ally) here. Use it. Breathe, lean forward or tilt your head towards the questioner and make eye contact. Find whichever physical cues work for you (which is part of the ongoing practice of noticing more about how you hold and use your body). Listen to the tone as well as the content. Notice everything you can about how it is being asked. Listen for the emphasis, or energy, or emotion — these are part of the question too.

Listening intently in this way gives you pause, and shows respect to the person asking (and their question). Slowing down brings you into the present and allows you to let go of shadow stories or expectations. This gives you a little bit of time to be with the question before you launch into a response. Even a few seconds makes a difference. It isn't enough time to think, plan or analyse consciously, but it is enough to allow your unconscious, which works much faster, to get going. If you really listen, you will find you have more resources to draw on than you might expect.

Listening also has a significant effect on the questioner. Sometimes, in fact, listening is *all* that is needed. Being heard and acknowledged is sometimes more important than receiving an answer. Many 'difficult' questions are, as we saw above, really about a desire to be seen.

Having listened, you are in a position to treat the question as an offer. Don't leap to conclusions about why the question is being asked, or judge the person asking it. Let go of whatever shadow story leaps up at this moment. The motivations and intentions of the questioner may be good or bad, but you cannot be sure of what they are, so trying to second-guess won't help you. Let go of all that judgement and, instead, simply regard the question as an offer. Which means finding a way to use it.

As ever, regard something as an offer and it becomes one. There are lots of ways to use a question or objection. Try answering a question with another question (which, coincidentally, is another improv game). For example, you might say:

— What makes you ask that?

— Does anyone else have the same question?

— Who is best qualified to answer that?

Such responses show you are taking the question (and the questioner) seriously and are trying to get to grips with their issue, rather than give a glib answer.

Unlike presentations, where most people keep their thoughts to themselves, in workshops people sometimes get very aggressive and say things like, 'This is stupid, it's a complete waste of time.' Years ago, this kind of response would bother me, but now, perversely perhaps, I like it. There is tons of energy and emotion in such a comment and the person making it is normally being both brave and honest. Which is a great offer.

For the person objecting (and for the rest of the group), it is powerful if you can accept their response rather than trying to argue with them. Accepting doesn't mean agreeing with them. I might ask why they think what we are doing is stupid, or a waste of time, or what it would mean to not waste time. There is no need to make them wrong. Who knows, they might be right and, through inquiry, I might be able to change or adjust what we do to good effect.

Often the fear of objections or questions comes from an excessive focus on 'getting through' your stuff. But it is pointless getting through your stuff unless your stuff is getting through. If you are only talking to yourself, you aren't communicating, however tranquil it may feel or however polished it may come across. Questions and objections to what you are saying allow you to get real-time feedback and you can adjust accordingly; then you are really communicating.

It seems to me there is a great irony at the heart of the difficulties we have around communication. We want to create a connection with people and yet we devise all sorts of shields and barriers, like Powerpoint, to protect ourselves from them, which creates distance. Communication isn't easy but, at heart, it is a very simple business that we tend to overcomplicate. Improvisers have given us a number of specific tools. These can help us communicate better in formal settings, like presentations; more importantly, they give us a way of working that makes the basic building blocks of communication both visible and comprehensible. The modest set of ideas and behaviours expressed in the basic practices is of untold value. Apply it to your communication and you could be using it all day long for the rest of your life.

Kirsten Gunnerud — *A place of confidence*

Kirsten Gunnerud is a facilitator and strategist focused on creativity, curiosity and experiential learning. She is the founder of Rocket Trike Studios.

For me, this started a scary 20 years ago. I had quit my job and moved to Utah, I was sleeping in a friend's room and had no idea what I was going to do. I came across a workshop Robert and Gary were running and somehow I just felt I had to be there. And I don't know why.

It has been an incredible thing for me. It has been a foundational piece in everything I do. It informs all my work, how I interact with people, how I parent my children, the kind of things I try to teach them and have them work from.

When we build our skill set around the three circles — notice more, let go, use everything — we get this ability to navigate pretty much anything that shows up. For me, this has turned into a place of confidence. I can say to myself, 'Okay, I don't like this, I don't want to be here, but at least I have the tools to figure out what to do with it.' These practices help balance everything else that we've been taught.

Different people use the practices different ways. For me, *notice more* is what I am most naturally attuned to. I love to work with it because so many people my age have been taught *not* to notice. Yet there is so much magic, so much to work with all around us. When I tune people into that again I see immediate shifts happen.

This has many layers. There's noticing more with our brains, there's noticing more with our physical senses, and then beyond that our intuition, our deep sense of things (even if that doesn't always make sense). And a lot of those, we are taught to shut down.

For people who are struggling or stuck, I'll have them do a 'notice more' journal, and I'll direct their noticing towards the beautiful little things that happen all the time, whether it's something as simple as a butterfly flying past, or watching the sunrise — it doesn't matter. Just that kind of noticing can transform someone's experience in a few minutes.

Letting go is harder — at least for most of the people I know — but so useful. For example, with kids. They have a lot to deal with, like the mean things that other kids say and do, so it can be incredibly useful to help them think about letting go of things.

With my kids, if someone has said something horrible, we first look at why someone might have said that (so that's a *noticing more* thing). And then if we realise that this kid might be hurting, or trying to be popular, we can start *using everything* and see that there might be reasons why they are doing these things that have nothing to do with my kids. And then we come around to the *let go*, which is that you don't need to take this personally, you don't need to take that in because it actually doesn't belong to you. So I use it to talk about a difficult situation with my kids.

There is so much for us to let go of. You can let go of feeling you have to be professional and adult and serious and perfect and right, let go of your title, let go of who people might think you are... the list is endless. Just show up, and be in this, and see what happens. If we can do this, we get to learn something and grow. We walk out better and happier in the process. And how often do we get to do that?

4
Creativity

Creativity sets humans apart. Everything we make or do depends on our creative history. From stone axes to supercolliders, the ability to create, for ourselves, is one of our defining characteristics.

From axes we moved on to fire, arrows, pots, agriculture, cooking, recipes, cuisine, nouvelle cuisine and so on, all the way up to the celebrity chef. Along the way we created language, art, science, philosophy and rubbish bags with little drawstrings that make them easier to close (one of my personal favourites). By being creative we have shaped and fashioned the world around us to an enormous extent. Creativity is an important part of what makes us human.

If creativity is our past, it is also our present. In our everyday lives we constantly face threats and opportunities we cannot anticipate, that require (or invite) a creative response from all of us. The pandemic that was unleashed in 2020 brought that home in a dramatic way, on a large scale. It is more obvious than ever how important it is to be able to adapt. There *will* be another pandemic: and it won't look like the last one. We won't be able to cut and paste from the past, so the kind of future we have will depend upon our capacity to be creative.

We also have to find ways to clear up the mess produced by the industrial 'solutions' of yesterday without producing yet more toxic waste, squandering energy or destroying the ecosystems on which we depend to grow food, cycle water or produce oxygen. Just doing less of what we currently do won't be enough. To navigate climate change we need to be creative on a scale that has never been seen before. The problem is vast, complex and new, so we don't have the solutions — we have to create them.

In a 2006 TED talk that has received 72 million views, Sir Ken Robinson, then Emeritus Professor of Education at Warwick University, argued that creativity is the new literacy. It is *that* important. In a global economy, driven by rapid technological change, creativity at every level is fundamental. Organisations of all kinds, including governments, businesses and NGOs, constantly need to serve people in new ways as their needs and interests shift. They might have to create new services or products, find new ways to deliver old ones or reinvent themselves completely.

The same is true for individuals, who need to be creative not just to keep themselves employable but in order to shape their lives, which will not proceed along the predictable, professional paths that they used to. As Robinson points out, most of the children in school today will do jobs that haven't been invented yet. This hasn't happened before.

Furthermore, all the most interesting and important human dilemmas, like how to reconcile liberty and security, are problems that we never 'solve'. Instead of settling on single answers, we have to come up with a stream of creative responses, as we adapt anew to changing circumstances. The world does not stay still, we are forever responding to all the complexity of life.

Creativity isn't just about solving problems either. It is important to the quality of our everyday experience. Being involved in a creative process brings joy and delight to those participating as well as those who benefit from it. This is not the sole preserve of artists or Nobel Prize winners. Psychologist Mihaly Csikszentmihalyi, who has dedicated his career to the study of happiness and creativity, argues that 'to have a good life it is not enough to remove what is wrong with it'. Happiness, it seems, is about more than solving problems. In order to be happy, we need to find ways to express and develop our creativity. Creativity, it turns out, matters an awful lot.

Co-creation

Given this importance, it is worrisome that the popular image of creativity is about as misleading as it is widespread. Ask most people to conjure up an idea of someone creative and its likely they will come up with a version of the 'eccentric inventor' or 'artist in his garret'. The image is of a lone individual, of rare talent, engaged in a tortuous process of creation, with inspiration occurring in blinding flashes.

There are two striking features of this image. First, it is not a very accurate depiction of how creativity occurs, either in the arts or in science (or, for that matter, in business). Secondly, it depicts creative people as 'other'. They are disconnected and separate.

If this is the image you have, it is unlikely you will think of yourself as creative. Which is inhibiting. It stops you being, or becoming, as creative as you might. To paraphrase Henry Ford — if you believe you aren't creative, you'll be right. We need to debunk this image.

Let's start with the pain. It may indeed be difficult to make a living as an *artist*, but that doesn't mean the *creative* process itself is a necessarily painful one. Struggle may be involved, but in many ways, play is more important to creativity than pain. Improvisers have an enormous amount of fun while they create. It's a large part of why they do it.

The idea that you are born creative (or not) is another unhelpful one. I often hear professional creative people promote it. This is hardly surprising, since it makes them 'special'. However, for those who aren't professional creatives, it sets up a self-fulfilling prophesy. If creativity is an innate talent, you would be a fool to try and develop it, so, lo and behold, you don't.

It is more helpful to think like the ancient Greeks. They suggested that people were 'visited' by the muse. For centuries, inspiration was a touch of the divine. It came and went. It was neither a talent, nor a possession — it wasn't yours alone.

In fact, this is much more accurate than creativity being regarded as a special, individual talent. Creative people rarely work in isolation. There is always a milieu — a movement or a community of some kind, where ideas are sparked off, exchanged, cross-fertilised and tested. This may be informal, like the coffee houses of 17th-century London, or formal, like the modern scientific peer-review process, but one way or another, there is interaction between people and their ideas.

This is very obvious with improvisers, whose creative process is visibly collective, but even when someone appears to be isolated, they still interact with other people's ideas, through reading or correspondence. It is neat and tidy to attribute acts of creation to individuals (and it may suit the individuals concerned), but there is almost always a collaborative element. The individual is always in a context — and ideas emerge from the relationship between the people who operate in that context.

If creativity is to become the new literacy, we have some work to do. Using improvisation as a source of inspiration is a good way to challenge many of the assumptions we make about creativity. It also provides some specific pointers about practical things we can do to develop our creative abilities. I am going to explore four of these:

1. The importance of play
2. Creative doing, not creative thinking
3. Putting flow first
4. Embracing constraint

Let's have a look at each in turn.

1. The importance of play

The Comedy Store Players have been performing an improvised show to satisfied paying customers once a week since 1985. This adds up to thousands of hours of relentless creativity. There are groups like this around the world. Improvisers reliably and consistently deliver a highly creative product over long periods of time.

If this ability were mercurial and mysterious, there would be nothing to do but sit back and applaud. Yet improvisers draw on a body of knowledge that enables them to do this. It is not luck or accident. The question is, what can we borrow or emulate?

Improvisers mostly perform comedy. Which means that they tend not to take themselves too seriously.

They are happy to play around. The rest of us should take note. We tend to take ourselves (and our work) more seriously. We think of ourselves as responsible adults, doing things that matter, which you shouldn't mess around with. It can easily feel like we don't have the time, the energy or the permission to lark around. That is a luxury we left behind in childhood. Being playful is not part of our self-image, or our job description.

If you want to become more creative, you need to change that. Or at least be willing to let it go from time to time. John Cleese has suggested that creativity is not so much a special talent, as a willingness to play.

Play is more than just fun (though we will get to that). Play and playfulness are important because they open the door to new possibilities. New ideas are always strange at first. Through play we explore what they might have to offer. We flirt with the unknown.

Allow yourself to be playful. Write yourself a permission slip if you like. Entertain ideas that you would normally dismiss, even if it is only for a few moments. Using 'everything' includes those things that might seem silly, so keep new or unusual possibilities 'in play' and see where they take you.

Don't cling on too tight to knowing what you want or you will never allow yourself to discover anything else. If Alexander Fleming had, he wouldn't have discovered penicillin. How do you know whether something will become relevant? Allow a playful attitude to loosen you up, to help you 'let go'. When supervising Master's students, it is those who have their dissertations completely mapped out in advance that concern artist Steve Chapman, who asks, 'Where is the space for learning or discovery then?'

Play around with things at the edge of what is normal or known. Read a magazine you would never normally pick up. *Rabbit Owners Monthly* will show you a whole world you didn't know existed (and thus, if nothing else, the limits to your own). Speak to someone you don't know. Ask a five-year-old for advice. Subscribe to a newsletter that has nothing to do with your work (and delete the ones that do). Eat different food. Allow yourself to wander off rather than always 'pushing on'. Look up. Look sideways. Meander. Fertile territory often lies in the margins or overlaps. If you are too direct, or in too much of a hurry, you will never come across them.

Playfulness also helps you to stop self-censoring your own ideas. If you are only 'playing' it doesn't matter how you come across. It is easier to stop worrying about whether you sound stupid. Musicians jam and lark around until something emerges. In Peter Jackson's documentary about the Beatles, *Get Back,* you can eavesdrop on the moments where songs you have known your whole life emerged through play (fuelled by remarkable amounts of tea and toast).

That play can be fun is a plus but it isn't the only point. Play invokes and engages the whole person: left brain, right brain, body and all. It connects us to other people, so that we build relationships as well as ideas. Our efforts add up. The load is shared. Energy and laughter are released. Improvisers understand these principles and embody them in their work.

For example, Gary constantly asks himself, 'Am I enjoying this?' He regards joy as a perfectly valid measure and believes that if he is having fun, then he will be more effective. 'Are we having a good time?' is the key metric for the work we do together on 'The Everyday Improviser' (in fact, it is the only metric).

If he isn't having fun, he will change what he is doing. This doesn't mean giving up, or going off in a huff, it means asking himself how he could act differently to make things more enjoyable. This requires presence of mind and discipline. It also requires being willing to be changed, i.e. being prepared to be wrong. The result is that Gary has a better time at work than anyone I know.

By contrast, for most of us, fun is a barrier. It makes us see play as trivial, or childish. We believe that we shouldn't be happy, or have fun at work, or only when we have 'earned' it. When I work with senior leaders, it is striking how many of them are uncomfortable and suspicious of play. As a result they enjoy neither the play itself, nor any of its benefits.

This attitude owes something to puritans and engineers, both strong influences on modern culture. To puritans, work is virtuous whereas play is indulgent and sinful. To an engineer, 'play' is looseness in a mechanism, so too much of it can be a bad thing. No wonder we find it hard to engage in play.

If you want to become more creative, a willingness to play, or be playful, is something that you can cultivate, individually and collectively. This means being more curious and open-minded, finding unusual sources of inspiration. Not as a distraction or a reward, but as part of the work itself. Given the public image of play, that takes commitment and a certain amount of courage. It's a tough job, but somebody has to do it. It might as well be you.

2. Creative doing, not creative thinking

When people in organisations talk to me about creativity, they normally talk about creative thinking. But what really matters is creative *doing*. It doesn't matter how creative your thoughts may be, if they don't translate into action.

You need to cook a meal or find a way to mend the fence. At work you have to make new packaging, or get people to behave differently when they answer the phone. When we built our house I learned that many of the most creative ideas weren't in the plans, but emerged from the act of building. The hand was as important as the mind.

To be creative we have to do something, not just think or talk about doing it. Creativity is embodied. It is physical, not abstract. You can't be creative just by thinking. Even for mathematicians, the physical act of writing equations on the board is important.

People get hooked on creative thinking because it is much easier to think about something than to do it. They also assume that thought is primary. That to act creatively you must *first* think creatively.

But improvisers know that isn't true. They know it is as effective, if not more so, to *act* yourself into a new way of thinking. Acting first doesn't mean being thoughtless or foolhardy. It means doing things before you know precisely how they work. It means physically committing to an action and allowing ideas to emerge. Nietzsche, himself a great thinker, suggested that all great ideas are conceived by walking. Since body and mind are integrated, not separate, ideas can just as well flow from the body to the mind as the other way round. Both paths are valid.

Actors will step into a scene *before* they have an idea. They may make a gesture or movement, without defining what it is that they are doing, either to the audience or to themselves. Only when another actor says, 'Looks like you're having trouble opening that tin,' do we discover what it is (or to be more accurate, what it has *become*).

By committing to the action we allow someone else to add their own interpretation, which may be one we would never have thought of. Thus we get creative. Together.

You want new ideas? Don't sit at your desk. Walk the factory floor or visit the shop. Phone your own customer service line and see how you get treated. Get your hands on the product (or your competitors') and play around with it, so that you really get to know it.

Reframe consumer research as action not talk. Instead of testing ideas with 'consumers', find the people who use the product a lot. Don't ask them what they think, watch what they do. Or better still, join in and play around with them yourselves.

A group of male car engineers, who were designing a car for women, did exactly that. The women suggested that one of the engineers acted out a woman getting into her car (for fun, they insisted it was the one who had a beard). When the bearded 'woman' walked up to the (imaginary) car and put his (imaginary) handbag down on the ground while he unlocked the car door, the women all exclaimed, 'You don't *ever* do that!' This prompted a creative conversation about issues of security, ways of unlocking the car and so on. Making the action visible created possibilities that would not have occurred if they had only talked about it.

Acting first also means not trying to anticipate. Anticipation slows things down. It is much better to try stuff out. Make a model or a prototype as soon as you can and see how it works. If what you make isn't tangible, design an experiment or game, instead of a model. One way or another, play your idea out. Learn from the experience. Incorporate that learning, then make a new prototype.

That's what design studio IDEO, one of the world's most creative companies, does. They make prototypes of whatever they are designing as soon as they can. Their motto is 'fail early, fail often'. If you want to be creative it is much better to focus on 'safe to fail', which means small-scale experiments with rapid feedback. This is very different from a focus on 'fail-safe', where caution and conservatism predominate.

Years back I worked as a consultant for a drinks company on new product development. The desire to be sure about everything made it painfully slow. There were umpteen rounds of concept development and consumer testing. Meanwhile, in a backwater of the same company, a few ingenious souls would mock something up, take it down to a bar and see what flew. Not only were they the ones who came up with the ground-breaking innovations, but they had a blast doing it. I wish I could say the same.

These renegade drinks developers knew what improvisers know — that the importance of creative thinking is exaggerated. If you want to get creative, don't just sit there and think about it, do something.

The easiest thing to do is move. It is also, quite possibly, the most productive. This is the direction I most frequently give people in workshops. It is often the *only* direction I need to give people.

When you move, a lot happens. You see things from a different angle. The light falls differently, different sounds reach you, you touch a different surface or feel a different movement of air, with a different scent or temperature. You receive a wealth of new information. When you move, you shift your point of view.

You change your internal environment too. Blood pumps and muscles contract. Your senses, which are only really interested in change, become more alert. Millions of nerve cells fire. Different sensations lead to different feelings. Changing your posture or position changes what you receive, and how you perceive it. This all happens very fast. It is automatic and powerful.

Sit in a different chair. Stand up. Lie down. Walk around

the block. If you want a more creative meeting, move people around. Don't let them get comfortably stuck in a particular chair, or their ideas will get comfortably stuck as well.

If it feels too strange to do this explicitly, be sneaky. Have frequent breaks, move furniture, disturb the physical layout so that people can't stay put, sit somewhere else yourself (to create a domino effect) or break them into groups or pairs for conversations. Variation and physical movement help people stay alert as well as increasing the chances of them having a new idea.

A beautiful example of the power of movement (and being playful) is a TED talk by John Bohannon about dancing your PhD. In a moment of playfulness, a scientist invited some dancers to help him communicate his ideas physically. What starts off as a means of illustrating ideas turns, quite unexpectedly, into something more powerful. In order to bring the ideas to life, the dancers, with their focus on the physical body, had a very different point of view to the scientists and started to ask questions that none of the researchers would ever have thought of. This input changed the direction of the scientific work itself and gave the scientists new insights and ideas. Which just goes to show, when it comes to creativity, it is all very well having a powerful brain, but there's nothing quite like a good body.

3. Putting flow first

People often say, 'There is no such thing as a bad idea.' I beg to differ. There are plenty of bad ideas. I know, because I have them all the time. We all do.

What is important is not to judge ideas as soon as they appear. If we judge ideas immediately, we don't just kill them, we kill all the other ideas they might give rise to.

Which is why animation studio Pixar's philosophy is 'from suck to unsuck'. This acknowledges that the first ideas are likely to 'suck'. I think this is more helpful than the claim that 'there is no such thing as a bad idea', which I find wrong-headed and cheesy.

Instead, I prefer to say, 'There is no such thing as a good idea ... *yet*.' This suggests that no idea is born complete. The '... yet' is important. It puts the emphasis on what we *do* with ideas, which takes the pressure off the idea itself. Whether your first idea is good, bad or indifferent, it will still need to develop, evolve, maybe even transform. An idea, like any living thing, needs to grow.

Improv actors achieve this by paying attention to flow. Their first instinct is to get going. They know that the audience wants to see something happen, so they take whatever they have and use it to begin their story. If they have an apple they take a bite. Or stuff it in the mouth of the pig they are roasting. Or use it to discover gravity, or tempt Eve.

What they do is less important than the fluency with which they do it. They know and understand the importance of momentum to the creative process. They appreciate that ideas can evolve very quickly once you create flow.

Filmmaker Robert Rodriguez works in a similar way. 'If you sit back and don't move; if you try and imagine how you are going to do the whole thing, you are already seeing obstacles that you don't want to face and you are not going to do it. Something magical happens when you just move forward.'

Trying to know everything leads to paralysis. Agonising over whether something is perfect or not will hurt you and the process (as the word 'agonising' itself suggests).

At the heart of this is the practice of accepting. To accept an offer is to take something, thereby acknowledging it, and do something with it. This generates flow. You extend your hand, I shake it. You tell me you lost your job, I commiserate (or congratulate you, depending on the circumstances). Accepting an offer connects two ideas, builds on them and leads to more possibilities. It gives impetus to the process. It acknowledges and includes other people by using their ideas, rather than ignoring or marginalising them. This encourages them to make more contributions. This is just as true at the family dinner table or in a business meeting.

If you accept ideas rather than block them, they have the chance to go somewhere. You set in motion an evolutionary process. Your first ideas become the parents (then grandparents and great-grandparents) of a great number of other ideas. This is why it is important not to judge them immediately. When we knock an idea on the head, we kill all their offspring too. It sounds brutal, but it's true. We need the fluency that accepting ideas brings, because the best way to make sure you have good ideas is to have lots of ideas. Accepting is neither passive nor weak. There are plenty of different ways you can accept any particular offer, as the example with the apple above demonstrates.

Thinking of ideas as parents of other ideas also reminds you that, just as we do with our own children, you have to let them go, stop trying to control them and see what wants to emerge (which is easier if you regard them as a gift from the muse in the first place).

This is particularly true once ideas start to get fleshed out. The creative process doesn't stop just because we have started to make something (or 'execute' in the rather morbid business jargon). We have to be prepared to keep on letting go because during the process of realisation an idea may be transformed further, often to good effect.

Leonardo da Vinci made many preparatory sketches for

his paintings. Yet his idea of preparation was very flexible. He wrote about the importance of not being wedded to an initial idea and continued to develop his ideas while he painted, so that the final work might be very far from the early studies. Art historians find it hard to say at what stage his work stops being preparatory.

Leonardo was also famous for failing to 'finish' many of his works, which has much to recommend it. During a creative process, leaving thoughts or ideas unfinished does two things. It invites other people to finish them. In doing so, there is a good chance that they will add something you hadn't thought of, and enrich the idea in the process. This takes the pressure off you, because you don't have to shoulder all the responsibility, which in turn allows you to become more fluent, more open and less controlling.

Tracey Camilleri, a colleague of mine at Oxford, describes herself as a 'half-a-sentence person'. She constantly invites you to add something of your own to complete her ideas, which makes collaborating creatively with her easy.

Accepting is vital to the creative climate. When ideas are habitually or routinely blocked, it crushes the people that contributed them, as well as the ideas themselves. Accepting creates flow and that takes you somewhere. If you don't like where you are, but you stay in flow, you will get somewhere else soon enough. By contrast, blocking stops you where you are. It cuts people and ideas off from one another and can produce confusion, even conflict.

To be fair, blocking can be an important behaviour, just not when you are trying to generate new ideas. It comes into its own when you are winnowing them down or trying to reach a conclusion. But it isn't the place to start.

The simple lesson from all of this is that if you want to become more creative, it is more helpful to focus on getting going, before you worry about getting it 'right'.

4. Embracing constraint

Improvisers are fond of making things hard for themselves. Not only do they do without a script, but they embrace additional constraints, which seem to make their task more difficult. For example, there is a game called 'last letter, first letter'. This is a scene where each new line of dialogue has to start with the last letter of the last word used by the other actor. So if I say, 'I can hear the plane,' you will need to start whatever you say next with an 'e', such as, 'Exactly, I told you they would come.'

This gives you some structure to work with. It might seem perverse, but think about what the constraint obliges you to do. To know which letter you have to use, you must wait for the other person to finish what they are saying. That stops you planning and forces you to listen. It gives you a start point, which cuts down the number of options you have to choose from. This creates a constructive climate and makes it easier to build on each other's ideas.

Though it is used on the stage, and I am using it here to illustrate a point, you can literally use this game in conversation, at home or at work, and it will change things. Even a few minutes playing this can improve the quality of the conversation that follows. People slow down, listen better and interrupt each other less.

Improvisers understand that creativity is stimulated by embracing constraint, not by a complete absence of constraints. In the arts, it is often the materials used that present limitations and constraints — whether it's clay or canvas or the sound of a sax. In their book *A Beautiful Constraint*, Adam Morgan and Mark Barden explore how constraints function as an engine of innovation in business.

The imposition of a constraint stimulates creativity because it provides something to create friction. Many years ago, composer Sidney Sager told me that he had to work with the limitations of the violin or the oboe. 'And if those constraints didn't exist,' he said, 'I would have to invent some.'

Creativity is about making choices, and when you can go anywhere it is much harder to choose. In workshops, when people get stuck it is not because they can't think of anything to say or do. It is because there are too many things they could say or do and they are paralysed by choice.

This is even harder when we obsess about making the 'right' choice — by which we normally mean the one that will make us look good (or clever, or funny). Embracing constraints gets beyond these unhelpful pre-judgements about whether your idea is a good or a bad one.

Understand this and it becomes easier to be creative. Don't flee from constraint, learn to use constraints constructively and seek them out. Let's try it now.

I need ideas for a talk I have been invited to give (about my book *Do Pause*) at an event in Washington, with a small but influential audience.

Now, let's take an everyday object that is to hand. I am going to take the coffee cup that I have here on the table. We are going to use that as a constraint to get new ideas. Here's how. We forget, for the moment, about our issue, and focus on the coffee cup.

First, we list the attributes and qualities of the coffee cup — plain, obvious things. I am also going to introduce another useful constraint here — time. You will have to take my word for it, but I get one minute, no more, to list whatever comes to my mind about the coffee cup.

Here goes.

White, round, drips, rings, sediment, dregs,
container, handle, everyday, hot, distraction,
everyday, leftovers/dregs, smooth, drug, ceramic,
hot, narrow, cheap, simple, round.

It doesn't matter that I repeated some words — what matters
is letting them out quickly. Here comes the creative bit.
You take these words and collide them with your issue.

Remember, my issue is ideas for an important talk. I ask
myself, 'How could that be white? What would it mean if
that were white?' I have to let go of being literal, ignore the
fact that it sounds like nonsense, embrace the constraint
and force it on to my issue.

This only takes a few seconds. Starting with 'white' sets
off a stream of consciousness that went like this:

White, white noise, snow, Erling Kagge, silence (could
I use sound design, or silence, to represent pause?),
Walter White from Breaking Bad *(what about video*
or film clips? Pause in popular culture?), white sheet
of paper, blank sheet of paper, white space (I should
say things I haven't said before, start from a clean
sheet, go beyond the book itself) ...

In a few seconds, it generates another creative constraint
— not to say anything I have said before. Which would be
a powerful discipline to work with. It also gives me some
thoughts about the form — using silence deliberately,
or maybe getting my son Bruno, who is a sound designer,
to work with me on it.

That was only the first word from the list, and it took
much longer to type this up than it did to do (even though
I type quite fast). It doesn't give me answers, but it gets me
going and gives me new starting points.

So if you want to get new ideas, find a way to embrace constraint.

— Connect or collide constraints of different kinds into your issue. Use whatever you have to hand, from a coffee cup to your children, or a two-hour deadline.

— Wide-open vistas are less fruitful than combining things that normally don't go together. Ask, 'If the mafia ran our company, how would they act?'

— Instead of bridling under a constraint, push it further by asking, 'If we had to cut the time and budget for the project in half, what would we do?'

— Use people that don't know or share the conventional assumptions. Ask the sales director about R&D or the R&D people about a sales issue.

— Use constraints in time. If you have an hour to come up with ideas, don't design an exercise that lasts an hour. Do six different exercises for ten minutes each, or the same ten-minute exercise six times.

If you can do this, it not only fuels your creative process but it changes how you feel about constraints. Instead of being problems you start to see them as offers, which is perhaps the single most creative thing you can do.

The last two years have been among the most creative of my career. With the pandemic in 2020, all of my work was cancelled. Embracing the constraint of technology helped me create two different projects and a whole new livelihood. It also means my carbon footprint has dropped dramatically as I no longer have to travel for work.

At first I resisted this. It took a while for me to let go and consider my options. Once I did, 'Yellow' (which is now my main occupation) burst into life. I realised that technology allowed me to work with people all over the world, over long periods — in contrast to the limitations of a physical programme that lasts only a few hours, or days.

I also noticed some traction to videos that I posted on LinkedIn. Inspired by how yoga teacher Lucas Rockwood was using short videos, Gary and I created 'The Everyday Improviser', a course that gives you a playful experience of the practices I am writing about here, in five short sessions, spread over a working week.

I had wondered about working online for years, but was sceptical. The constraint was what created the possibility, but only once I chose to embrace it.

Improvisation suggests that if you want to become a more creative individual, you need to be less of an individual. That, in a sense, all creativity is co-creativity. While this is a generalisation, it is a useful counterpoint to the prevailing impression that creativity depends upon possession of a special talent that you have, or lack, from birth. It releases you from the burden of having sole responsibility for your own creative powers and shifts the emphasis on to how you interact.

Understanding what improvisers do tells us a lot about the conditions that enable a group to act more creatively. It gives us a little of the grammar for the 'new literacy' of creativity we need. Improv suggests that by becoming more playful, more focused on action and flow, and more willing to embrace constraints, you will become a lot more creative. Improv groups show us that, in the right conditions, anyone who wants to can make a creative contribution. Which is just as well, given how many contributions are needed.

Steve Chapman — *Don't try*

Steve Chapman is an outsider artist, speaker and facilitator, creator of the world's only silent podcast and the Inexpert 2018 conference.

I think the purpose of the human experience is to paint your imagination into the world. I see every moment as an invitation, as an offer. I think every piece of work I'm doing now starts from that moment of asking, 'What's the offer here, what am I being invited to play with?'

For example, in 2018, I saw something on Twitter about a leadership hacks podcast and I thought, 'Why has everyone got a podcast when they have nothing to say?' I went for a run and asked myself what would be the opposite. I realised it would be nothing, a downloadable pause, empty digital content. And what if it had special guests that I sit with and people download the silence? You can see the 'Yes, and…' with the universe going on there.

Two and a half years later, I had 100 episodes of 'The Sound of Silence', the world's first silent podcast, with guests including Eddie Izzard and Terry Waite. It started with frustration. When stuff goes right, or wrong, the only question I ask is, 'What's the offer here?'

The world doesn't normally work like this, so I set myself traps. One of my mantras is 'start before you are ready'. When I got back from that run I registered the domain 'Sound of Silence' and announced it before I had even thought it through.

Up to the age of about 11, I was into all of this without knowing it. And then I forgot about it. From age 11 to about 30 — 'the wilderness years', I like to call them — there was a numbing out of these creative invitations. I thought, 'That's not what adults do, I should put that to one side.'

The seeds of shame are sown early in life. We can be playing, immersed in stuff, then all of a sudden, something happens to pull us out of that and we are reprimanded, told that it's wrong. We learn we mustn't trust that spontaneity if we want to become a functioning adult.

You need to let go of the illusion of certainty and control that thinking the conventional way gives you, but it *is* an illusion, it isn't real. This can be quite difficult.

I think there is an accidental (or maybe subtly intentional) numbing of what it means to be a creative human being. It might not suit those in authority if everyone was able to liberate that creative, subversive, artistic self, and express themselves in ways that are powerful.

When I left the corporate world, I remember that my entire body was saying, 'Right, time to leave,' and my head was going, 'No, no, no, don't be stupid.' It would be too reductive to say it's a physical sensation; it is an instinctive calling, an absolute gut feeling, a learning to trust spontaneity.

For me, it's really reaching back into that childlike (not child*ish*) intuition. It is not impulsive. I don't suddenly run across the road with my eyes shut, because that intuitively doesn't *feel* like the right thing to do.

It isn't about making art or coming up with something good. We are all constantly improvising and adapting. Creativity is that constant dance and adaptation with things as they are.

Most of what we do to get unstuck gets us more stuck because it's coming from that same philosophy. Don't try to get good, just relax and let go. Don't try at all. Just be open to the invitations that are already there.

—

somethingsidid.com | *canscorpionssmoke.com*

5
Leadership

If an alien were to land in the middle of an improv performance and say, 'Take me to your leader,' the actors would be stuck. Even if they were cool enough to deal with the appearance of little green men on stage speaking English and spouting clichés, the request to identify a leader would floor them.

In improvisation, there is no designated leader. There is no commander, CEO or president. No head honcho, top dog, big cheese or padrone. So what can improvisation possibly tell us about leadership?

As you might expect, I am going to suggest that the answer is 'plenty'. The reason is that you don't need leaders for there to be leadership. A formal position in the hierarchy, with a corner office, flashy car and big title, guarantees nothing. You may have worked for someone who has the position (and the trappings that go with it) but displays no leadership. As Professor Kurt April of Cape Town University puts it: 'I have met many CEOs that I wouldn't follow to the toilet. And many people on the shop floor that I would give my life for.' What we are interested in here is leader*ship*. That elusive ability, wherever it comes from and whoever displays it, to inspire and move people to do things they wouldn't otherwise be willing or able to do. Understood this way, leadership doesn't only happen at work but in families, groups of friends, or any other collective of human beings that comes together to do something.

Improvisers routinely display that ability. They perform under pressure. They are exposed and highly visible. They have to cope with uncertainty and rapid, unpredictable change. They have to interact and connect with the ideas of other people. They know how to create a climate where people feel engaged and appreciated. These are all leadership behaviours and improvisers are good at them.

It is the behaviour of leadership that we are going to focus on in this chapter. We will look at what it is that improvisers do that we can learn from, in order to develop our own leadership capabilities in organisations, or in everyday life.

This isn't just about work. Parenting is the original form of leadership and, for many of us, it is also the arena in which our leadership skills are put to work, or challenged, every day. The most important leadership role you ever play may have nothing to do with your job.

Anyone can lead

As our little green man discovered, on the improv stage, there is no single leader. This is the first thing we can learn from improvisers — that leadership can be something everyone does, whatever their position. You don't have to wait until you get promoted; you can start now. On stage it has to be this way. No one is put in charge and the characters that actors play emerge from the action itself. Everyone must actively participate so that ideas come from all quarters; no single perspective is enough. The success of the whole depends upon connecting these different contributions in a coherent way. Everyone is responsible for creating the conditions where the work gets done; no one can do it on their own.

Improvisers have a fluid approach to leadership. Different people have to be able to lead at different moments, as the situation demands. People must be willing to step up, or step back, as the circumstances require. This means paying close attention and being highly sensitive to what is needed. It also means being willing to let go of your own agenda and ego. Not only does everyone have an *opportunity* to lead, but if the group is to fulfil its potential, everyone has the *obligation* to lead, when required.

This isn't unique to the stage. I once had a former soldier in a workshop. He observed, wryly, that in combat 'the person leading is the person who can see best'. The same idea is in play in the famous Toyota Production System, where any worker can stop the line. Every individual, at whatever level, has the chance to lead and the power to exercise it. The person who sees best, leads.

If this is an advantage in manufacturing, in a knowledge or service business it is vital. There is more information than anyone can absorb, so you need to be able to take advantage of many points of view. If leadership is concentrated in one individual, or even a few, you become vulnerable.

Another military example serves as a striking illustration of this. Within days of the D-Day landings in June 1944, American officers were wearing their helmets back to front. This was not bravado, it was to hide the white lines that officers had on their helmets. The German forces had quickly learned that without officers the American troops didn't know what to do, so they issued orders to target the officers, who as a result took very high casualties.

The American officers realised what was happening and started to wear their helmets backwards, so the white stripes were less visible. This shows how concentrating leadership in a few critical nodes (the officers) made the system as a whole more vulnerable to shocks. Turning their helmets around was a logical step, but what the Americans really needed to do was develop more distributed leadership.

This is a challenge. The idea is disappointing or threatening to anyone, little green man or otherwise, who believes that a select group ought to have a monopoly on leadership. The figure of the heroic leader is a powerful and widespread idea that has acquired the status of a myth. It suits wannabe heroes because it makes them feel important. It suits the rest of us because it allows us to duck responsibility. We have a significant bit of letting go to do.

Viewing leadership through an improviser's eyes poses some uncomfortable questions. If leadership is lacking, it forces you to look at yourself and do something about it, rather than lament the shortcomings of others. You must ask what your own contribution is and how you might show more leadership yourself.

This does not imply that roles don't matter, or that some people don't — by virtue of their position or experience — have more responsibility than others. What it does mean is that no one has a monopoly on leadership and that each of us can make a difference. As US President Theodore Roosevelt said: 'Do what you can, with what you have, where you are.'

Leadership as a practice

You cannot learn to improvise from a book any more than you can learn to swim in a library (which is why I put so much emphasis on practice). Improvisation is an embodied ability. It draws on the whole person. Physical sensation, space, position and gesture are all important, as well as reason, emotion and intuition. This means that it has to be developed through experience and experiment.

Leadership is also a practical endeavour. An academic or purely intellectual approach is too narrow. It won't help you to motivate people, or handle uncertainty. Reading about it is different from doing it and leaders with impressive experience can be underwhelming when you hear them talk. They might be able to do it, but they can't necessarily explain it.

This means that if you want to develop your leadership ability, the focus of your efforts must be on your own experience. By all means take ideas from leaders (great and small) and from books (including this one), but make sure you put them into practice for yourself, in your own context, and see how they play out. Only you can find out how they work for you. You must lean into experience, not shy away from it.

This can be unfamiliar and uncomfortable. In our culture, people talk a good deal about making mistakes but in general, errors aren't applauded. We are trained to avoid taking risks and rewarded for doing so. Hollywood is a great example of this ambivalence — it claims to be all about creativity, but in fact is deeply conservative. It's an attitude summed up by the saying: 'Everybody wants to be the first to do something for the second time.' Such attitudes are widespread.

Improvisers, by contrast, are braver and more philosophical. They accept that discomfort is a necessary part of what they do and embrace it gracefully, instead of ignoring it, wishing it away or struggling against it. When I asked one performer how they dealt with being in such a highly exposed position he said, 'You learn to get comfortable, being uncomfortable.' A skilled improviser is not someone who doesn't get nervous, but someone who doesn't let nerves paralyse them.

We would do well to develop the same capacity in our approach to leadership. Rather than reaching for answers or becoming paralysed by the fear of making mistakes, we should accept the discomfort that comes with the territory and learn to become comfortable, being uncomfortable.

One source of comfort is the idea of practice itself. Faced with an infinite and unpredictable set of possibilities, improvisers do not plan or theorise. They practise. Through experience and experiment, on stage and in workshops, they develop a repertoire of behaviours that stimulate, frame and channel how they respond.

Thinking of leadership in terms of practice is a gift. But just as 'practice' is a noun, 'practise' is a verb, and carries, built into it, the idea of an activity that is continuous and never-ending. A practice is something you do and keep doing. No matter how accomplished you become, you keep at it. The notion of a practice thus cultivates persistence.

The endless nature of it means that, taken to heart, the idea of a practice can take you far. Nonetheless, it is also realistic — by accepting that you need to practise, you acknowledge that you do not have the answers. It releases you from the insidious idea that you ought to be perfect. Whatever level you are performing at, you continue to practise. Which means that when setbacks occur you do not lose heart. Having a practice makes it much easier to act in the midst of difficulty. You may get confused, but you don't get derailed.

This allows you to become more compassionate, particularly to yourself. The emphasis shifts from trying to avoid mistakes, to learning from them. Instead of, 'Is it right?' you start to ask, 'Does it help?' Framing leadership as a practice also starts to erode the unhelpful notion that it is an innate ability. It can't be, or you wouldn't be able to practise it.

So what does it look like to have a leadership practice? Imagine you are lost or stuck and people are looking to you to lead the way. You don't know whether to go on or go back (either literally, or metaphorically). There is plenty of doubt and uncertainty. The pressure is building and you need to act. In such circumstances there is a risk that you will fall back on familiar responses, such as blame or denial. Most often we simply work harder, as if more effort were the answer to every predicament. These responses come all too easily, particularly when we are under stress.

In these circumstances this practice can act as a discipline that guides you. You can ask one, or several, of the three basic questions (or some variation of them). You know the ones:

1. **How can I notice more?** (This will slow you down, help you see things or people you are missing, encourage you to lean into your senses and help you become present, etc.)

2. **What can I let go of?** (This will encourage you to notice and question assumptions, expectations, invisible rules or personal agendas.)

3. **What else can I use?** (This will enable you to reframe problems and find new resources.)

Asking these questions gives your mind somewhere to go, other than into a spin, especially when you are under pressure, or people are looking to you for guidance. It centres and calms you. It suggests how you might usefully direct your attention. It doesn't need to be the only thing you do, but whatever other ideas or theories you choose to play with, you immediately have something to act upon. It is an obvious place to start when you are stuck or stymied.

A practice acts as a compass to help you navigate the inevitable discomfort. It won't make difficulty disappear, but it can help you find your way through it.

For example, imagine you have to give the result of a poor performance review to someone. One leader we worked with, faced with this difficulty, focused on noticing more. Rather than plan how to present the bad news, she decided to put more effort into paying close attention to the other person. When she did so, she found that the person she was reviewing would often raise the issue themselves, which made it easier for both of them.

The practice can guide you when you have no idea what to do (something that happens more often than most leaders care to admit). When Commander Mike Abrashoff took over the USS *Benfold*, it was a warship with low morale and poor performance. Some parts of the ship were 'no-go' areas for officers.

He started by talking to every crew member. He had no idea what would come of it, but reasoned it would give him something to use. He was right. He invited crew members to tell him about the things that frustrated them. He found there were plenty of changes (about food, small-arms practice or painting the ship) that he could implement immediately. This made it more than a PR stunt. The changes he made showed that he wasn't just *talking* to them, he was *listening* to them as well. There is nothing more motivating than seeing your words acted upon, and as word spread through the ship, more and more ideas were heard and implemented.

'Be changed by what you hear' is an instruction that improv directors give their actors. This is a lot more effective than trying to listen 'better'. If you want to demonstrate you have heard, you have to listen, otherwise you don't know how to react. Being visibly altered leaves other people in no doubt that you have listened. Which is why Abrashoff's application of this simple practice had such an impact on the ship.

Noticing more also means paying attention to 'weak signals'. On the improv stage a small detail often develops into the main story. For this to happen, the actors have to notice it, act on it, and be willing to let the story develop in a very different way than they may have anticipated.

In business, new ideas and developments — whether threats or opportunities — often appear from the periphery. A new competitor from a completely different category unexpectedly appears, or a small-scale technological development turns out to have the potential to transform your business. Developing the ability to perceive these 'weak signals' is a fantastic leadership behaviour. Make sure that you pay attention to people and ideas that lie outside the mainstream, in forgotten or neglected departments or functions. Can you notice the responses of the quieter people in your organisation, who often see more than they say? Noticing the 'weak signals' that lie on the periphery can alert you to growing threats and help you find new opportunities.

I was recently asked which of the three practices is more important for leaders. Though it is always going to depend upon the particulars, in general, I would say that noticing more is particularly important. Paying attention to the people you are leading is an act of generosity.

When you pay proper attention to someone, you give of yourself. Quite literally, you 'devote' your attention to others. People feel this, which makes them more inclined to follow you.

A mark of a great leader is someone who, however important they may be, still pays attention to others. They have 'presence'. They make the people they are leading feel seen and heard. Masters like Mandela can elevate this to the level of genius. In an age when technology seduces us into a state of 'continuous partial attention', striving to be more present is one of the most important things you can do. Don't be put off by the fact that it sounds dull.

No more heroes

Leaders face challenges to which there are no established answers. Or to put the same thing another way, if you already know the answer, then even if it is important, what you are doing isn't leadership. So leaders need new ideas. Since other people will see things you don't and have ideas you won't, you need them to contribute.

Using other people's ideas requires humility. But a leader who is willing and able to take ideas from anywhere is strengthened, not weakened.

Sometimes it doesn't take much. Leadership is often about connecting what is already there. You don't have to be perfect, or know everything. You don't even have to be the smartest person in the room, you just need to be willing to use what shows up.

We see this in storytelling games where, often, all that is needed to make sense of the whole is someone to simply add an 'and' or 'because'. As one participant put it, 'Sometimes all you need is a conjunction.' Having the humility to make a modest contribution shows you are serving the story (or whatever your collective endeavour is) not yourself. Improvisers value 'connective tissue' highly and this is another tip we can take from them. Finding opportunities to connect ideas and people is a wonderfully simple yet extremely powerful piece of leadership behaviour. It may not make you stand out, or look impressive, but that is a good thing.

By serving the story, rather than yourself, you generate trust. Psychologist and executive coach Jon Stokes says that the more self-centred you are, the less people trust you. Which means that being seen to serve the story isn't just noble, it is a good leadership strategy. People will trust you more as a result.

As a facilitator, I need people to trust me. Particularly because I invite them to do unusual things. Working in that context has taught me that, as a leader, there is a lot you can do physically, rather than through talk.

I once had a small group at Oxford who were resisting sharing anything meaningful. One day I set the chairs up in pairs, facing each other and uncomfortably close so that people would almost be touching knees when they sat. As a result, when they came in, no one did sit down. We then had a conversation about why that was. It got them talking about how they felt, which was exactly what I had wanted. I used the room to do the work for me.

Sometimes you respond physically to things as they emerge. I remember one instance when a game went 'wrong' because one of the participants forgot the instructions. I was about to step in and correct her, but instead, curious to see what would happen, I simply leaned back against the wall, relaxed and smiled. All I needed to do was be 'fit and well' about it and the group were happy too. They found a different way to make the game work, without me intervening, and the experience fuelled a debrief conversation that was far richer, because of what had gone 'wrong'. This is what it means to hold a space.

Working with uncertainty

Many years ago I met Gene Kranz, the flight controller on Apollo 13 (Gene was the character played by Ed Harris in the movie). Partway through the journey to the moon, there was an explosion of some kind on board the spacecraft. Despite having no idea of the cause, or the extent of the damage, Kranz and his team in Houston had to make certain critical decisions with the eyes of the world upon them.

Kranz talked about what to do when uncertainty prevails. 'You have to act before all the data is in,' he said. 'If you wait you would never actually get all the data, because you would lose the spacecraft.' In the face of uncertainty, you must act. This requires courage and, as Kranz explained, a willingness to trust weak or diffuse data — otherwise known as intuition.

Improvisers become very practised at acting 'before all the data is in'. They focus on getting going, rather than getting it right. In a situation where you don't know what an answer might look like, this makes a lot of sense. Once you get going you get feedback. You can then adjust or change accordingly. Try nothing and you are none the wiser. Momentum is also motivating.

Putting the emphasis on getting going doesn't mean that you don't care where you go. As a friend of mine is fond of pointing out, 'When you shoot from the hip, you still aim.' My favourite metaphor here is that of a boat. Unless you are moving forward through the water you are at the mercy of wind and tide. Get going and you can steer.

However, when I say this in workshops, people often protest. 'How can I start before I know what's going on?' they ask. It is a deeply ingrained habit. Yet leadership always involves unknowns. The mistake is to assume that because you don't know everything you can't act.

You will never know everything so, by that logic, you would never act. You need to give up the idea that you are, or need to be, in complete command of everything. Trying to be is what stresses you out, or paralyses you. The territory of leadership is the unknown.

If you are paying attention, you always have something to go on. Emotion and feeling are data too, albeit of a different kind, below the threshold of conscious rational thought.

Through practice, improvisers develop a sense and feel for which offer to accept in order to get moving. Learning to read subtle patterns, including your own feelings and responses, is a skill that can be developed. Improvisers do it all the time, as indeed do many senior business leaders, who use intuition more than is often supposed. For example, Sir John Templeton, financier and founder of Templeton College, Oxford, would often make significant investment decisions based on feel, not reasons.

There is plenty to practise here. We have to let go of our attachment to certainty, particularly in the form of conscious rational knowledge. Forget the idea of anything being 'futureproof'; the only thing we can be sure of about the future is that it will surprise us. We need to understand and accept that valid information shows up in many ways — such as sense or intuition — not just in numerical data. We need to develop our sensitivity, or ability to read these diffuse signals, and we need to be willing to act upon them, notice what happens and adjust or change as a result. That should keep you busy.

Creating the climate

In nature, all waste is food. There is nothing that isn't useful to somebody else. Just ask a dung beetle. What a wonderful trick that is. Improvisation's very own version of this elegant ecological truth is that everything is an offer.

Take that idea into the leadership realm and you create a different climate immediately. And creating the climate, or conditions, is a large part of the work of a leader. This is an incredibly constructive way to reframe problems, errors and failings. Whatever it is, it isn't a problem, it's an offer. Putting the focus on looking for offers is contagious. Good leaders do it instinctively. When Thomas Edison's disheartened foreman reported to his boss that they had tried a thousand different materials for the filament of a light bulb with no success, Edison replied that this wasn't failure — they now knew a thousand materials that didn't work and they could use this knowledge to help them find one that did. Edison didn't have an answer, but he did have a way to motivate his people to keep looking for one (which they eventually found).

There is a physical practice that helps with this, which improvisers call being 'fit and well' (rather than 'sick and feeble'). It means being physically balanced, open, grounded and relaxed in the face of difficulty and uncertainty. This is the embodiment of the practice of seeing everything as an offer, and is empowering. You can start in your body. Adopt this physical attitude and you become more likely to be able to deal with the difficulty.

Ingvar Kamprad (of the chicken feathers) is another natural. One IKEA manager told me a story about a time when they ordered too many wardrobes. Ten thousand too many. Everyone was nervous about telling Kamprad, but when they did so he was delighted. Instead of looking for someone to blame he immediately engaged with the question of what to do with 10,000 wardrobes. This attitude seems to have rubbed off throughout IKEA, whose willingness to see everything as an offer allows them to end up selling cardboard roof racks or opening up their warehouse to customers. Enabling people to see mistakes, problems and errors as offers is a constructive piece of behaviour that creates a positive climate.

Unsurprisingly, this 'keystone' practice is of enormous value in leadership. It is also a brilliant way for a leader to work with people's objections. In some way or other, leadership involves change of some kind and there will always be objections to this change. Normally these are seen as obstacles or barriers, and it is easy to take against the people that raise them. It can become personal.

It is much more productive to see objections as offers too. One successful innovator from a large and very conservative company said that whenever someone said no to him (which they did, frequently) he just interpreted it as a request for more information.

Alfred Sloan, CEO of General Motors in its heyday, went looking for disagreement. He would adjourn board meetings where he thought everyone had agreed too easily 'in order to generate some constructive disagreement'. He was worried that people were just telling him what they thought he wanted to hear and was wise enough to know that opposing opinions were vital to the health of the organisation, so he encouraged them.

They say that you can tell the quality of an organisation by the speed with which bad news travels upwards. If you see objections or opposing opinions as offers, then you can improve the quality of your organisation at a stroke by creating a climate of trust, where people share information of all kinds, instead of trying to guess what the leader wants to hear. Doing so enables you to understand other points of view, show up gaps in your knowledge, or simply give you a read on how people are reacting.

Being willing to see objections as offers is a way to generate 'constructive dissent', rather than the 'destructive consent' that prevails when people aren't willing to speak up against those in positions of power.

Status

When people interact, they are constantly adjusting their position relative to each other. This is going on all the time and is independent of your formal position (which is fixed). A child can comfort a parent. A duke may ask his butler for advice. Improvisers call this flexible position 'status'. Your status, in this sense, depends upon your behaviour in the moment. It can shift up or down very quickly.

Improvisers use this understanding to help them create scenes that are credible and engaging. This constant ebb and flow of status is a natural part of human interaction.

For anyone interested in leadership, understanding that status is flexible and separate from position is a profound insight. It lays bare one of the fundamental dynamics of relationships and gives you a whole new dimension to work with. Whatever position you are in, you can play high or low as circumstances demand and shift instantly. This gives you a way to be sensitive and flexible, to modulate your behaviour, to act according to the context, rather than letting your role dictate how you should act.

Simply understanding that status is always in play is valuable in itself. It will help you to see when you confuse status with position. But we can go further. Improvisers can tell you what to do to shift your status up or down and what the benefits of doing so are.

To play high, or raise your status, you can:

— Be definitive ('There are two important points here ...')

— Invoke authority ('I saw in the *Financial Times*...')

— Draw on exclusive experience ('When we started this business ...')

There are certain physical cues that raise status automatically: speaking in an even, measured tone, pushing your chest out and, curiously enough, holding your head still while talking (if you don't believe me, try it!). This isn't a comprehensive list, but you get the idea.

To play low, or lower your status, you can:

— Be self-deprecating ('I know a little about this')

— Express doubt or uncertainty ('I am not sure what this means')

— Elevate others ('Jane is the one who really understands Nigeria')

Physically, you lower your status by moving or fidgeting, fluctuating the speed and volume at which you speak, or by adopting a lower position than someone else (e.g. sit in a lower chair). Again, there's more, but this captures the gist of it.

People normally assume that a leader has to play high status. This is a mistake. Think about it. How do you feel about people who always act as if they know it all, who are uniformly decisive and determined? Do you warm to them? Do you trust them? Would you willingly offer up your ideas and energy? In short, would you choose to follow them?

This is ironic, given that many people feel that being impregnable, knowing everything and trying to be perfect are pre-requisites for a leader.

In fact, playing high status has plenty of downsides; we just tend to ignore them. High status distances you from people. It is exclusive, in the negative sense. It is not engaging, nor does it encourage people to take initiative. It can be intimidating. However impressive it may make them appear, someone that relentlessly plays high status will pay a price for that inflexibility.

Low status, on the other hand, which we might assume is a weak position, has advantages, which we also tend to miss. It breaks down barriers, generates empathy, defuses tension and can be very charming. It is inclusive not exclusive. In an era when collaboration and creativity are of increasing importance, when complexity means that we face more unknowns and faster changes, these are important qualities for a leader to cultivate.

Of course, low status in excess can appear weak, but a complete absence of low status actually makes you more vulnerable, not less.

Thus the improviser's understanding of status offers two extremely useful lessons for the practice of leadership. First, by pointing out that there is a dynamic element in how we position ourselves relative to other people, it opens up a whole new dimension for us to work with. We need not be taken prisoner by our position. On occasion, junior people can play high status and senior people can play low status to good effect.

Secondly, it gives us a palette of possibilities that we can learn to use skilfully and sensitively, according to the particular circumstances. High and low status both have advantages and disadvantages. If you understand these, whichever formal position you occupy, you can practise raising or lowering your status from moment to moment according to what you feel is required at the time. This invites you to be playful with status, rather than feeling you are bound by it. It allows you to try different ways of acting and see what happens as a result. Which, in turn, helps you not to take things (or yourself) too seriously.

Beyond the script

The ability to flex and adapt is absolutely central to the work of leadership. Harvard Professor Ronald Heifetz, one of the world's most respected leadership thinkers, says, 'Leadership is an improvisational art. You may be guided by an overarching vision, clear values, and a strategic plan, but what you actually do from moment to moment cannot be scripted.'

Improvisers have a lot to offer us when it comes to the moment-to-moment business of what we actually do. They show us that leadership is not the special preserve of elites, but an ongoing practice we can all engage in. They offer us a few simple ideas, like listening and seeing things as offers, that may not seem very grand, but which, in fact, go to the very heart of leadership. They also invite us, through an understanding of status, to develop a more sophisticated and flexible way of relating to the people we are endeavouring to lead.

This is a mighty relief. The work we must do to develop our leadership is actually very simple. We do not have to know the answers and there is no need to try to be a hero.

Hugh Derrick — *The leader is not the expert*

Hugh is a partner of challenger brand consultancy eatbigfish.

A lot of the work we do is with large groups. Standing in front of a group you are leading is a daunting experience. When you feel nervous and you manifest that, it transmits to the people around you. The participants don't want to see the facilitator fail. They want to feel that someone is managing the energy of the room, so transmitting confidence is important.

It may sound odd, but one of the things I have learned from improvisation is about how to prepare. The concept of being 'fit and well', of being physically open, still and grounded, is really useful.

An audience in a workshop is often sceptical. They are saying to themselves: 'What am I doing here? I hate workshops. They're all crap.' You have a limited amount of time to gain their trust and attention, so those first few minutes are critical. So 'fit and well' is really helpful language to me, even if you're not feeling great (which you might not be). If you can manifest that, it pays back in spades.

You are in service of the group. You can't be worrying about the projector, or yourself, or how you'll look. You have to be able to respond in the moment. If you are rushing into a meeting room thinking about other things, you can't do that. It is really obvious if your attention is somewhere else.

There is a kindness and generosity to this — it means really actively listening. The other thing is that sense of being fully present, so that you are able to accept whatever happens and not be put off by it, to see everything as an offer.

We want a group to solve its own problems, to get excited about things, to be more capable collectively than they are individually, so we have to be able to transfer energy and give them the space to do that.

In this context, the physicality that comes with improv is important — everything from where you stand to how you use silence. You can learn to work with those things.

There are people who need to be drawn out. If you only stand at the apex of a group, and never move towards them, that's not going to happen. They say you shouldn't turn your back on people, but sometimes that can be useful (to close someone down). Or stepping out of the group and standing behind them, so that they have their collective gaze on what they've created (not on you).

We normally use a U-shape of chairs, and no tables, so people have no barriers in front of them. That, and moving people around the room regularly, creates a sense of community.

Sometimes a boss won't come to the whole session, but just pop in at some point. If they sit at the back, or apart, this can create a completely different dynamic. If that happens, we would bring them physically into the group. It comes down to being aware of a space as an offer.

Body shape is also interesting. I had one colleague who was incredibly flexible. She would squat down, literally using a low status physicality, when she wanted to get the group to talk, giving voice and authority to them.

Learning to use silence is incredible. If you can hold it, someone will fill the vacuum. And what they say will probably be more interesting than anything you were about to say. You need to hold the silence for what you consider to be an awkward amount of time, and then keep holding. The way to do this is to count. Think of a number that feels testing. Then double it.

One of the joys of our work is that, even though we are leading the workshop, it is not our job to be the expert.

Other people in the room know more about beer, or the law, or whatever it is we are working on, than we do. Once you are comfortable with that, you know that expertise is all around you and your role is just to access it.

Sometimes people are disruptive. As a facilitator, you have to deal with this like a stand-up comic deals with a heckler. You can become the mouthpiece of the group, but you have to keep serving them. If you react personally, then you get it wrong.

You need to have fun with it, because facilitating is exhausting. The fun comes from realising you've gone through a day where your audience's energy has sustained you. Yes, you are giving them energy, but you are also getting energy back from them.

Underlying improv there are really interesting thoughts that you can learn from. You can't have it all go smoothly, you need to stumble past stuff, and then come back to it. In our world, where leading a group means soliciting insight, and getting contributions and opinions from the floor, everything really is an offer.

—

eatbigfish.com

6
Everyday Improvisation

When I first started working with improv, people mostly asked us to do idea generation or presentation skills. They assumed that if it had a useful application at all (and many were sceptical) it would be related to creativity or performing in public.

That isn't wrong, and in these pages I hope you will have found some techniques to make your brainstorming sessions or presentations more lively, but there is more in play here than a few neat tricks to come up with new ideas or engage an audience.

Over time, the value of an approach like this became more widely appreciated. I have spent many years, at Oxford and elsewhere, helping people develop their capacity to respond to complex change creatively. That might sound grand, but in practice it means obvious things like paying attention to different people, letting go of assumptions or the desire for control, and working with whatever you have at hand. Many of these people have told me they found the ideas just as useful at home as at work.

Then, with the pandemic that began in 2020, it was impossible to deny the importance of adaptability and improvisation. Changes that would have taken years were happening in days. Teams who, on Monday had never worked virtually, were all online by Friday. People began to say to me: 'We are all improvisers now.' My inner response was that we always have been, but I kept quiet. If the need was more visible, that was good enough for me. However, it is important not to think those circumstances were unique, something we can forget about once we are no longer in crisis.

Charles Darwin himself is reported to have said: 'In the long history of humankind (and animal-kind too) those who learned to collaborate and improvise most effectively have prevailed.' It turns out he didn't, but whoever did say it, the idea is an important one.

The unimaginable complexity of life means that collaboration and improvisation are always necessary. Nothing living, from a bacterium to a blue whale, has a script for their life. This includes you. Somehow or other, every living being copes without a plan and always has. As Kevin Kelly, founding executive editor of *WIRED* magazine put it, 'No logic, except *bio*-logic, can assemble a thinking device, or even a workable system of any magnitude.' Life is too entangled for anyone to ever be in control of much for very long.

Our analysis leaves out the irregular bits. The misfits. The outliers. The mess. Anything that cannot be controlled is, by definition, excluded from a randomised controlled trial. The emotions that drive us are omitted from the calculation of rational self-interest that our economics sets so much store by. The trouble is that the mess — that unruly, complex, fluid bundle of interconnections — is where we all live.

The improv theatre is like a laboratory for the mess — it is a place where you can study how improvisation works and thus, in a sense, how life works. No one intended this, but it happened anyway, which rather neatly illustrates the point. To paraphrase basketball coach Phil Jackson: 'There is more to life than improv theatre: but then there is more to improv theatre than improv theatre.'

The practices make visible what is going on in our communication and relationships, which is why I use metaphors like 'x-ray machine' or 'fundamental grammar'. There are games to play, a language you can learn and tools to apply in any context you like. The terms are ordinary and everyday, which makes the ideas easy to remember. Naming them 'into existence' gives a sense of legitimacy: once we have the words, they become 'things' we can work with.

The managerial fantasy

However, the fact that there is improvisation in everything can still be hard to see, because the story we tell ourselves about the way the world is, is so strong. This dominant narrative presumes that control is not only possible, but desirable. It isn't. Author Chris Kutarna calls this 'the managerial fantasy' and it shows up everywhere in our organisations. Underlying all the noise about personal productivity and time management is a similar illusion — that if only we had the right system, we could get our time and our lives under control.

That we fall for this doesn't mean we are being stupid. The emphasis on measurement, analysis and control is deeply woven into the way we think and talk *because* it has been incredibly successful. It has worked extraordinarily well, for hundreds of years.

Given our technological success and the material well-being it has brought, it makes sense that we have all been educated in this way of thinking. That education is reinforced every day by the language we use and the culture we are part of.

The trouble is that it has become so successful that we have forgotten it is a way of thinking at all, and mistake it for 'the way things are'. We take *a* truth to be *the* truth. This is not an error that slower, older, gentler cultures tend to make.

But any way of thinking is partial and limited, however successful it has been. No single lens will enable you to see everything. As psychologist James Hillman said, 'The ideas we have, but don't know we have, have us.' Science, as well as religion, has the potential for fundamentalism (though it tends to be more subtle). When we treat life as a form of machinery, it isn't surprising that we end up stressing ourselves and damaging living systems.

The ideas we have been exploring here offer us a different way of looking at our lives. Which is disturbing. Literally. They upset many of the things we take for granted (which is one reason why it takes practice to embrace them).

For example, the idea that you can have order without control is a radical thought. It runs counter to everything we have been taught. It questions the wisdom of working so hard to organise and plan everything. But just as improvisers shape their stories without ever being in control, you can do the same.

Imagine you come home from work exhausted and there, teeming with energy, is a toddler, eager to play. Instead of trying to invent something clever, just start to play and see what emerges. I remember an occasion with my eldest son, who was then less than two. He gave me a ball, so I threw it. He brought it back so I threw it somewhere else. Quite quickly it became an intricate game of deception and deceit. I didn't need to plan, or be in control.

We created this game without deciding anything in advance. And my two-year-old did most of the work.

Another hallmark of the dominant narrative is our enthusiasm for breaking things down into bits. Taking an engine to pieces is a good way to understand it.* Taking a person to pieces in order to understand them isn't. Yet we do it all the time, without even noticing what we are doing, or what is lost in the process. The psychology I studied at university reduced what I felt about a piece of music, or a girl, to a sequence of cells firing. I am sure lots of cells were firing (especially when Mary Banks floated across the lawn), but life, as we experience it, is more than that.

For an improviser, there is too much information and too little time to break things down into pieces anyway (which is also true in most of our everyday lives). They learn to work with sense and feel, which are faster. Their instinct is to join things up, which is how they create the ideas and actions that drive their stories forward.

I have come across people that write a spreadsheet to analyse which house they might buy. That might work as post-rationalisation but it won't tell you which house you love. Instead of trying to understand the bits, focus on the whole. You can practise this by choosing quickly in restaurants. Don't analyse the dishes, choose on feel. You will take less time, enjoy your food more and get practised at making more improvisational decisions.

Focus on building things up, not breaking them down. One great way to do this is to connect people together. I can't count the number of times that acting on a hunch to create a connection has led to a new friendship, opportunity or adventure. As Chilean biologist Francisco

---

* Although, as Aldo Leopold said in *A Sand County Almanac*, 'The first rule of intelligent tinkering is to keep all the pieces.'

Varela once said: 'When a biological system comes under pressure, the way to make it more healthy is to connect more of it to itself.'

Another barrier is the habit of dividing things into two opposing categories. This suggests that either you improvise, or you plan. It is a strong tendency and starts early. At my school, aged 16, everyone had to choose either arts or science. I wanted to do both. I was told this was impossible. It wasn't, but the staff were so attached to the categories they had invented that they could not see any other possibilities. Even the pupils joined in, tidily sorting themselves into groups of their own, which were equally separate. You were either sporty or clever. You couldn't be both. I played in the first XV at rugby and was in the Oxbridge stream. Where did that leave me?

You might think you aren't prone to this, but it shows up everywhere. For example, while working on this book I posted a picture on Instagram of my filing system, with neat rows of numbered sections, colour-coded to show how finished they were. I was immediately teased about using such a system for a book on improvisation. As if a book on improvisation should *only* be improvised.

Had anyone stopped to think about it, they would quickly have realised that you can't hope to organise 25 years of material without some kind of structure. But they didn't. Our responses are immediate and instinctive. We are so used to sharp and oppositional divides that we set ideas against each other, without even realising it.

Improvisation is not an alternative to analysis and planning. It is a complement. You need both. You cannot run everything by improvising, but you cannot run anything without it.

Take building, for example. You can't build without a plan, but you have to be able to adapt creatively along the

EVERYDAY IMPROVISATION

125

way or you will never finish, let alone get a good result. This is true whether you are extending the kitchen or building an Olympic stadium.

We spent two years building our house in Spain. I was already an enthusiast of improvisation yet even I was staggered by the amount of creative adaptation that had to be done on site by the craftsmen to correct mistakes, oversights or take advantage of opportunities missed by the plan. Many of the most distinctive and most pleasing features of the final building — like the porch, the cellar or the raised garden — weren't on the plans at all. They emerged from the work itself.

Travelling is another common example. If I ask you to tell me a story of a wonderful journey, or holiday, I would bet good money you will tell me about something unexpected or improvised. You are unlikely to tell me the story of something that went exactly to plan.

This doesn't mean you shouldn't plan your travel, but be prepared to adapt and change to what happens along the way or you run the risk of missing out. I once accepted an offer to hop a ride on a truck across the salt flats near Uyuni in Bolivia at ten minutes' notice. My plan had me heading in another direction altogether. Had I followed it, I would have missed walking across the border to Chile under the most incredible stars I have ever seen, or bathing in a hot spring while condors flew overhead. (Though it would also have spared me the schnapps-induced hangover the next morning, courtesy of the excessive hospitality of the border police.)

Improv without the games

I am easily seduced by novelty and easily get bored, yet after 25 years I am still messing around with these ideas. Which is surprising. In part, this is because I am always learning. I find new ways to set up, run or apply games I have been playing for decades. I learn from colleagues and clients, who do things I would never think of. All of which is great, but there is more to it than that.

The ideas have changed the way I see the world and live my life. They have become part of me — something I also noticed in the people I interviewed for this book.

The improvisational approach is compelling because it feels so alive. When I stop struggling against the flow of events and allow myself to participate in them, there is such joy and delight to be had. Things I could never imagine happen all the time.

I also love how forgiving the practice is. When I make a mistake, or behave badly, or get stuck on exactly the same thing yet again, there it is, waiting patiently, nudging me with a question that gets me moving. It is almost magical that such a simple set of ideas can capture so much of how life seems to work.

Looking back, I can see how these ideas were in play from the start. When I first met Gary Hirsch, it was to talk about his art, but he happened to make a passing comment about improv being a practice, which I noticed and latched on to. We both let go of the original agenda and explored that instead. I invited Gary to do some work with a client of mine, and he accepted the offer on the spot. A business, a great friendship and everything else I have written about followed. I could not possibly have planned all this.

A few years later I realised that the leadership programme I worked on at Oxford relied on improvisation on many levels, not just in the session I ran. The most important learning happened in the spaces, not the sessions — between the participants, in spontaneous conversations. The structure of the programme — the lectures and sessions — were important, but their role was to stimulate a response in the participants, which is what we worked with. The real content was what people brought, not what we gave them. We weren't trying to transmit information, we were creating an experience.

This is what I call 'improv without the games'. The Reading Weekends that I host are another example. The only elements I have a hand in are the venue (a beautiful old house) and who comes. There are only two rules: 'Read between meals, talk over meals'; and 'You can only have one book at a time'. Everything else is improvised — people choose what they read, who they talk to, what they talk about and so on. Yet despite the fact there are no learning objectives, no programme and the books are chosen at whim by the participants (not according to an agenda or theme) it is always a powerful learning experience. You cannot know in advance who is going to learn what, so you have to be prepared to let go of specifics, but that allows for discovery. As one participant put it, 'I find myself discovering answers to questions I didn't know I had.'

This works over a longer time frame as well. In 2020, unable to work in person because of the lockdown, I set up Yellow, together with Alex Carabi. Yellow is a five-month online programme. Groups of six people meet every two weeks for two hours. But that is about the limit of the structure. Everything else emerges.

This works on a number of levels. There is no programme that determines what we will cover in that period. Instead, Alex and I pay close attention and design each session as a response to the previous one. Based on what we hear and feel, we choose a question or invent an activity, which acts as a stimulus for the next session. Sometimes that might include a guest we think has interesting experience to share, but they are never 'subject-matter experts' — in part because the subject matter of Yellow is the people who come, and no one can be an expert in that (sometimes not even the people themselves). Sometimes we choose to complement what has gone before, other times we do something which contrasts with it. But there is no overall plan.

Within each two-hour session it is mostly improvisation too. We have a few elements of structure (like a check-in) that help us hold the space, and we have a start point, but what unfolds from there will depend upon how the group respond and the questions and ideas that occur to them. Sometimes we don't even get that far. In the chit-chat at the beginning, a theme may emerge that we notice engages the group and we decide to follow that instead, letting go of even the minimal plan we had.

This doesn't mean we don't prepare. We spend a long time chewing over each session and exploring possibilities for the next one. We are also always looking out for ideas (and people) that might one day be a useful piece of stimulus, but we prepare a broad territory, not a narrow path.

Letting go of the normal goal-driven approach isn't as unusual as it may sound. There are whole fields which incorporate something very similar into their normal practice, 'agile' software development, for example.

This is an approach where many of the elements of 'notice more, let go and use everything' are in play, even if that isn't the language they use. Teams review progress every day. Roles aren't prescribed. People work on what they have energy for. The structure is designed to provoke quick responses and new combinations, not exercise control.

Thus improvisational behaviour is stitched into the very fabric of the way things are organised.

There are plenty of other examples too, some of them famous. American manufacturing company 3M have, for decades, given people a time budget to work on their own ideas. Gore Associates (inventors of the famous 'Gore-Tex' fabric) concentrates on the human scale, and creates 'village'-sized wholes, of about 200 people, where roles are fluid and people don't have titles. Semco is a Brazilian engineering company whose structures are all about promoting interaction and autonomy and nothing about control. Semco sounds unique until you hear about Morning Star. Morning Star is the largest tomato-bottling company in California, yet its employees write their own job descriptions and set their own salaries. Sounds like there isn't much left to let go of.

During a takeover crisis, a steel company in Canada adopted three rules for meetings so they could make decisions quickly. The rules were:

1. The meeting decides.
2. The meeting is whoever is in the room.
3. The door to the room is always open.

That way, anyone could participate in the decision-making but you had to be there. Presence was what mattered.

One software company invited its designers to help each other with their own personal projects for a day. These were the things people had personal passion for, not work stuff. This is a good way to use what you have — your people and the ideas they already have energy for. It was a great piece of letting go too, because they did it with no particular end in mind — just to see what emerged. What did emerge, in fact, were ideas of such quality, with such energy behind them, that they decided to abandon their formal innovation process, which was cumbersome and ineffective by comparison. They adopted the improvised method, letting go completely and accepting the new offer, to create a new stream of flow. The net result was better ideas in less time and more motivated staff.

There are far more of these improvisational stories than we realise, for the simple reason that we don't tell them this way. We post-rationalise our success, misrepresenting and misunderstanding it in the process.

For example, Richard Pascale, a leading American business thinker, who I worked with at Oxford, tells the story of Honda in America. Their success was hailed as an example of brilliant strategy. Richard, who knew something about Japan, had a hunch this wasn't the whole story. He paid attention to that hunch and decided to spend some time getting to know the Honda people who had been personally involved. He got underneath the post-rationalisation and closer to the experience itself. He discovered that, in fact, strategy was not the source of their success.

Like Richard, Honda had acted on hunch and feel. They had made many mistakes and errors along the way. For example, choosing a model because its handlebars 'look like Buddha's eyebrows' didn't show much insight into post-war America. They did not plan in detail. What they were brilliant at was noticing what was happening on the ground and responding quickly. Often, without telling head office. Their success was due to their ability to adapt, which Richard called 'The Honda Effect'. Yet the business schools were trumpeting it as a triumph of strategy.

This isn't surprising. The dominant narrative looks for standard, unifying models, not anecdotal stories about maverick companies adapting to particular circumstances.

The trouble is, particular circumstances are what we all face. 'Anecdotal' should not be an insult. Such stories provide insight and inspiration into how we might design more organic, less mechanical organisations. They won't tell us what to do, but they can invite us into a productive exploration of our own.

This is not to say that improvisation alone is the answer. But it is a healthy response to the complexity of life. It recognises that uncertainty is something to be enjoyed rather than endured and invites you to engage in a different way — less push, more pause.*

Don't drink the Kool-Aid

Statistician George Box famously said: 'All models are wrong, some of them are useful.' I hope you find the model I have explained in this book to be one of the useful ones, but that does not make it right.

That might sound like a strange thing for me to say, but it is very much in the spirit of what I have been writing about. The idea that everything is fluid and contingent underlies this approach, so it would be perverse to insist that the language or the model I have used is sacrosanct.

In fact there is nothing unique about these ideas. I first became interested in them because they reminded me of the science of complexity. They connect, or overlap, with many other (wisdom) traditions, such as stoicism or Zen. So I would counsel you not to get too attached to any of the particulars (something I imagine a Buddhist would approve of).

---

* It wasn't until after I had written *Do Pause* that I realised the germ of that idea was already here, in this book...

Instead, I would encourage you to play around with them. Which, by contrast, is very much in keeping with the spirit of improvisation. One difference it does have, versus some other approaches, is that it is playful and light, so you shouldn't take it too seriously.

The practices won't tell you what to do anyway. They won't tell you what you should pay attention to, or let go of, or where the offer is in a difficult situation. What they will do is keep inviting you to ask yourself the questions, but you have to respond to those questions yourself.

This is important. In a session that was part of 'The Everyday Improviser', someone asked whether always being flexible could make you 'disappear'. As a woman, and an immigrant, she felt that she was always the one adapting to others and was worried that this approach would be too accommodating.

I could see what she meant, but in fact the model doesn't advocate one thing or another. It gives you some ideas to use consciously to get what you want. If you want to block ideas, or cut flow, in order to ensure you are seen (or for any other reason) then there is nothing here to say otherwise. It is up to you to decide what you want, in your particular context. Whatever it is, with practice, these ideas can help you get it.

I would also encourage you to mess around with the language. If you prefer 'opportunity' to 'offer', use that. If 'being present' is a more useful idea to you than 'noticing more', so be it. And though the three circles in the model may seem very tight, there is some wriggle room here too. For example, Kirsten Gunnerud (interviewed on page 68) prefers to put 'pause' at the intersection of the three practices, rather than 'everything's an offer'.

I love this, for a couple of reasons. First, it fits beautifully. Noticing more, or letting go, will automatically create a little pause. Or the other way around. As Lisa Kay Solomon says, 'When things are not going the way I expect, I can pause and apply the improv practices.' It flows both ways and integrates the idea of 'less push, more pause' into the model.

The second reason I liked it was personal. The book I wrote before this one was entitled *Everything's an Offer*; the book I wrote after it was *Do Pause*. So this version of the model neatly links the three books together.

I mention it here to illustrate that even though I came up with the model, I do not have the last word. Other people have changed it, or built upon it in interesting ways. You can do the same.

Wouldn't that be dull?

Improvising is the most natural thing in the world. We all do it. You are doing it now. Your eyes, skin, gut, blood and brain are all improvising, each on their own and all together. Like a forest, or traffic on our roads, or email traffic on the internet, or the food supply to New York City, the most stupendously complex flows are organised in a wonderfully intricate, improvised dance. There is no one in control. The global pandemic of 2020 brought this home in no uncertain terms.

Understanding this is a fabulous liberation. In the past, when most of what happened was way beyond our understanding, the dogged pursuit of control made sense. But not anymore.

I once ran a course called 'Sit Stretch Eat Play' with my friend Edward Espe Brown, which combined meditation, yoga, cooking and improv (hence the name). After meditation one day, Ed was musing on the question of control, which someone had raised: 'It's a funny thing to want really, isn't it … Because you could never achieve it, and even if you could … Well, wouldn't *that* be dull.'

The promise that once we get everything ticked off and tidied up, then we can be happy, is a delusion, and a dull one at that. Who would want such a life?

This doesn't mean giving up a way of thinking that has been so successful, but it does mean understanding its limits. A plan, or script, or recipe, will only get you so far. There are other intelligent responses that complement our existing approach. Improvisation is one of them. It doesn't just help you navigate the mess. It is a way to happily be in it.

Taking to heart a few simple ideas that improv offers us can shift how we go about our everyday lives and work. They help us to accept, with humility, that we play a small part in an incomprehensibly complex world. They help us to enjoy what uncertainty brings us, rather than always trying to close it down.

They give us some ideas about how we can hold ourselves while we move towards 'the more beautiful world our hearts know is possible',* which we cannot yet see, or describe. They enable us to reconnect with our own irreducible, improvisational nature and, most importantly, give us something practical and simple to do.

---

* *The More Beautiful World Our Hearts Know is Possible* by Charles Eisenstein

Johnnie Moore — *Deep improv*

Johnnie Moore is a tutor on the Oxford Strategic Leadership programme and works as a facilitator. He is the creator of Unhurried Conversations *and author of* Unhurried at Work.

There is a way that some people use improv I find very unsatisfying. I call it 'shallow improv'. It focuses on fun and games, it's a bit manic and 'happy-clappy'. I am not interested in that at all.

My feeling is that there is something else, you might call 'deep improv'. I read an article by the jazz pianist Keith Jarrett, who got deeper into what improvisation actually is. He writes of working by half-felt hunch, moment by moment. He feels his hands move to do something and then, when that seems too obvious, chooses to do something else. I think this is what I am trying to get to.

When I wake up in the morning, there is a whole list of familiar things I habitually get angry and frustrated about, that are unlikely to change. If I can catch this, I can ask myself, 'What if I don't follow this line of thought?' and change the subject. I might say (to myself), 'What's for breakfast?' which is more down-to-earth and connects to some kind of sensory impulse. This frees me from the chain of thoughts: 'should have, could have, what if, why don't they ...?'

When I wake I could describe myself as depressed or anxious, but it helps if I call it something else — a made-up name (like 'zagprog', for example). I look at it afresh and ask, 'What else might it be?' It works surprisingly well. I realise what I feel need not be anger; it might be energy or something else.

I feel better, but *not* because there is a solution. There's no problem-solving going on, there's just being present to what is. I don't do anything about it. It is a non-doing, really. We have these scripts, patterns in the way we respond.

Interrupting or changing those, choosing something else, maybe that is deep improv? What can happen if we make a different choice about how we respond?

Years back, I experienced something like this in encounter groups. The purpose of the group is to 'encounter' other people, to notice something that you want to explore, maybe challenge. In one of these someone was reciting a lot of information about the violence he suffered as a child. I noticed it was hard for me to pay attention. I spoke up. I explained that my mind was wandering and I was wondering if anyone else was having a response like that. Others said they were.

I was out on a limb — this was risky, but I had named an elephant. The speaker himself recognised that when he spoke of these experiences he often felt that nobody paid attention. The conversation we had after that was very different.

These moments connect to deep improv. You stick your neck out and say something that puts you, and the other person, out on a limb. And you don't know where you are going from there. There's something about the capacity of groups to contain all sorts of really powerful feelings and to switch from a tremendously tragic story one moment to something completely hilarious the next and hold it all in a container.

When I am challenged or stressed, I might look like I'm asking for advice, but actually I just need to know that someone is being really present. Close friends may find it hard to just *be* with us. Yet that is often what I need when I'm really struggling.

I think this is something to do with being so present that I can reconnect to the inner wisdom. To feel connected, and part of the field, and not on my own. Perhaps what I am calling 'deep improv' is just a way to reconnect to the networked fabric of life?

—

johnniemoore.com | unhurried.org

7
Game on

I want to close with a few more things you can do: some games. They encapsulate the practices we have explored in this book. They give you a concrete bit of structure, which can make them a good place to start.

This is the first thing to notice. The forms have structure. They aren't any old game, or *just* for fun. Nor are they competitions or puzzles – you can't 'win' or 'solve' an improvisational game. They give people an experience that is as varied as the people participating. They make visible what is happening, allow you to try different ways of acting and see what happens as a result. All in just a few minutes.

For example, the rules of 'Swedish Story' (see page 151) oblige the storyteller to accept the disconnected words their partner gives them. This means regarding obstructions as something to use. You quite literally have to take 'everything as an offer'. By doing so, you quickly discover how easy and empowering that can be, and how impressive it looks to an audience. The translation into everyday life — where things you don't expect or plan for constantly come at you, from all angles — is clear.

'Incorporations' asks people to form physical groups around common themes or questions. It uses the space in the room as a physical 'offer' to generate energy, create connections, map out ideas, or give feedback. This shows how moving our bodies, rather than just talking, can help us to work things out quickly and easily.

'One to Twenty' invites you to let go of systems, agendas and control, and to see what you can achieve as a group by being really present.

Below you will find brief explanations of these and a few other forms you can try out for yourself. You might use them to 'break the ice' or 'create learning readiness' in the academic jargon (something which may seem trivial but, in the thinner atmosphere of online meetings, is ever more important). Or, to shift the energy and mood, generate new ideas, or work on communication or negotiation skills. There is plenty to choose from.

Working by stealth

Whatever your explicit purpose, and whichever games you use, by playing them you are also introducing people to the practices as well, whether you choose to spell that out or not. You are working (perhaps by stealth) at a deeper level, giving people an experience of how productive and satisfying it can be to work in an improvisational way and of how much easier and more natural that is than they might suppose. You allow them to discover, through play, a different way to work, even a different way to be.

The games are a kind of container. They may not look as if they are connected to the everyday business of your life or work, but they *will* show something about how people communicate and relate. They may just seem like 'light relief' but that can be a virtue. The fact there is no 'content' makes how people interact more obvious.

You can see whether people really listen to each other or not, if they 'block', whether they build on each other's ideas and so on. The playfulness creates a climate where people are more open to new ideas.

A space to practise

This idea of a 'practice space' is a familiar one. Athletes train using exercises they would never use on the field of play. When musicians and actors rehearse, they don't just play the piece, or deliver the lines that they will later perform.

We need to have the capacity to deal in (and *with*) uncertainty without becoming paralysed, stuck or squandering all our energy and attention on trying to control that which is beyond our reach. This is an ability our formal education and training hasn't helped us develop.

This is hard to do on the job. An improv exercise is one way to grow that capacity, to feel what it is like, to see how you respond, where you are found wanting and where you have surprising ability. The beauty of these games is that they allow us to notice something about ourselves, and what happens as a result of how we behave. Playful though they may be, they invite us to take our own experience seriously.

Don't just play the games, play around with them

The explanations I give, which we'll come to, are simple and brief. This is deliberate. Lengthy descriptions are tedious to read and still won't cover most of what could happen. A detailed description also suggests that there is a 'right' way to do these things. Which there isn't. There are a few pointers that will help you set them up and get going, but no script for how they might play out. The point of doing them is to see what happens.

Nor should you take my explanations too literally. There is nothing sacrosanct about the games. Where one ends and a new one begins is hard to say, and doesn't matter anyway. Regard what I say about them as a start point, not an end. This is not a recipe, it is a set of ingredients ... and you are the chef. Add to them, subtract from them, bend them, twist them, adapt them, combine them, steal elements from one and inject them into another.

This is how new games get invented. They are created and evolve through the doing. They are the result of past play, honed through experience, embellished and elaborated by different interpretations, enriched by 'mistakes' and misunderstandings. They are the product of the practices as well as the embodiment of them.

There is a lot to work with here. You can find your own applications of these games as well as new rules or variants. You can play around with the set-up, add your own riffs, find new debrief questions or more economical ways to explain the rules. Feel free to mess around or make things up. I would love to hear what you come up with.

Many people I have taught them to have adapted them in ways I would never have imagined. Film director David Keating found a way to blend two walking games ('Walk and Stop' and 'One, Two, Three People Walking') so that they require barely any instruction. He simply starts playing himself and everyone else joins in by copying him.

Hugh Derrick, partner of eatbigfish, uses 'Yes, and ...' at the beginning of a three-day brand identity workshop, to demonstrate and model the behaviour that will be needed for the workshop to succeed.

Somatic coach Amanda Blake took the counting game 'One to Twenty' and used it to provoke 'difficult' conversations so that people could learn about how it feels to give feedback in tense situations.

So don't feel shy to make up your own versions.

You can also trust participants to be a great source of innovation. Sometimes, when you explain a game, someone will understand it in a different way than you were intending. Instead of correcting such 'mistakes', see if you can use them. They often turn out to be a gift. This also has a useful side effect — it stops you being anxious about doing it 'right'.

I remember once, when working with a new MBA intake (at Portland State University), one of the participants spontaneously added some extra information I hadn't asked for. This turned a simple name-learning game into a rich, complex story game. It doesn't always work as neatly as that, but groups are often brilliant at making things work one way or another.

Absurdly, some improv troupes try to 'own' (even copyright!) certain games, which to my mind runs completely counter to the spirit of this work. Holding things lightly and being willing to be changed by how people respond is part of the practice for the person running a game as well as the people participating.

So be prepared to let go of your plan or idea of how the game 'should' work: take whatever people have added, let it run and see what happens. This shows that you are willing to walk the improvisational walk, rather than sticking to the detail of your plan, which will impress the group. Indeed, showing that willingness might be the most important thing you do.

Can it not work?

When I started working with improvisational exercises
it terrified me. The first time I set out to run a workshop
I asked a friend, Scott Dawson, then Dean of the Business
School at Portland State University, what I could do if it
didn't 'work'.

'Can it not work?' he asked.

I immediately (and anxiously) blurted out: 'Absolutely,
it could be a disaster, what if they refuse to play?'

There was a lengthy pause.

'Would that be it not working, or would that be it working
in a way you hadn't anticipated?' he asked. This still helps
me now, over 20 years later. 'Can it not work?' has become
something of a mantra for me.

Use what you have

You can use these games in two basic ways. You don't have
to design a whole workshop. You can start small, and use
them one at a time as 'refreshers' to punctuate a gathering
of any kind. Run a single game either to kick off, conclude
or enliven a meeting, for example. Or to keep people
occupied during a delay.

When thinking about which game or games to play, by
all means think about what you want to achieve, but bear
in mind that most of the forms will demonstrate any of the
practices. They aren't *really* about anything in particular.

Pay attention to the practical details — like the physical
surroundings. How much space do you have, how easily can
people move around, what furniture is there? Think about
your audience requirements as well (remember these, from
Chapter 3?). Think about the context. What is the gathering

for, what else is going to be happening, how might a game enhance the experience?

The size of the group is another basic variable you can use to help you choose which games might work best. Do you want to do a whole group exercise to connect everyone, or give them the safety of working in pairs where there is less performance anxiety?

Using single exercises here and there, to punctuate a meeting, can be especially useful online. When the shift to online working started in the lockdown, I, like most of my colleagues, was sceptical and focused on what was missing or absent.

But as the situation continued, the practice itself came to my aid. I realised that my beliefs were limiting me as much as the technology. I needed to let go of them. What if I thought of the limitations of the online environment as offers? After all, if I had to run a workshop in a long thin room, I would ask myself how I could use the long thin room. Why not do the same here?

All of a sudden, things got a whole lot easier. In the game 'Presents', people can't literally give each other an imaginary present, but I can still put them in pairs and ask them to hand their partner a gift through the camera of their computer. This works remarkably well. They can see the size and shape of the present their partner is offering them, and take what they are given. And as a plus, passing stuff 'through' the camera adds an extra element of playfulness to the experience.

Once I started to think this way, I noticed there were fewer limitations than I had assumed. Many of the technological platforms let you arrange the 'room' so you can set up a common order on the screen. This allows you to play any of the games you would normally play in a circle (like 'Yes, and ...', 'Character Circle' or 'Word at a Time').

It isn't the same as working in person but there is more to work (and play) with than I had realised.

For example, people may be connected via technology, but they are still in a real physical environment, having a bodily experience, and there are plenty of offers there. Getting them up on their feet or moving around is totally possible, and even more important than it is when they are seated around a table in the same room. The tedium of hours spent staring at the screen means something incredibly simple can be of great value to shake things up (see 'Shake Eight').

You can also turn off cameras or microphones, allowing people to be unobserved, in the privacy of their own space. This allows them to lark around, to make whatever sounds or movements they like, however ridiculous — something they might not feel able to do in a room full of people. This phenomenon is called the 'disinhibiting effect of technology' and shows that, while there are undoubtedly losses when working online, there are also some gains.

The fact that people are often at home is another opportunity (or offer). A home environment is much more varied and personal than an office. Gary has used this to develop a whole series of exercises he calls 'Scavenger Hunts'. He gives people a very short space of time (less than a minute) to go and find an object. He might ask them to find something that they love, or hate, or don't know what it is, or why it is there, or that is the colour red, or that represents a memory of some kind. Then he will use that object to start a conversation, or tell a story, or act as a stimulus for new ideas (see 'Object Tap', page 153).

If you get more ambitious and want to run a workshop then I would encourage you to choose a number of games in advance but not stick rigidly to a plan. Prepare a territory, not a path. Pay attention to what happens and adapt accordingly.

Variation is always good — a loud game followed by a quiet game, a whole-group game followed by a pairs game. To be rigid about using improvisational exercises is contradictory and will undermine what you are trying to do. If you want to have an impact on people, you need to walk the walk.

Part of that walk is understanding that the games are not formulaic. Although there are consistent patterns, you never know how people will respond and something new can always crop up. Remember Scott Dawson's maxim: it may work in a way you do not expect.

This is important. If you play a game in order to prove a particular point, it is a way of trying to control people. If you can't let go of that, there is a good chance you will be tripped up, and people will interpret things in a way that will derail you. Let people have their own experience, whatever that is. Allow things to emerge and enjoy the fact that people see things in different ways. It keeps you learning and interested in the group, which is a boon for them, as well as for you.

You need to be clear about this, because participants won't be. People are used to being given puzzles or problems that they have to solve, and they tend to bring that attitude to this experience. I have even seen people trying to work out how to 'win' a game like 'Presents'. Be ready to remind them (frequently) that these games have no right answers.

After playing, people will often ask, 'What was the point of that game?' This isn't necessarily aggressive or critical (so don't leap into judgement and presume it is) but it often reveals their assumptions. They frequently want to know what the *right* answer was, i.e. what they were meant to take from the game.

How to deal with this could be a book in itself, but obviously, what you want to do is to treat the question as an offer. Do that and even if your questioner really *is* being cynical or deliberately provocative you will get something to work with. My instinct would be to ask them what *they* think the point was, not as a defence, but out of genuine interest. After all, there is a chance I might learn something new. They might well see something I don't and they might just be dying to say it — which gives you the opportunity to 'see' them massively, which will help engage them (remember the importance of 'seeing' the audience?).

Having done this I would then probably share what *my* purpose was (otherwise it seems like I am being evasive). And at some level, I *will* have something to say. It could be something as simple as: 'The point was to get you to move.' This may be different from the kind of 'point' they had in mind, but we can then explore that difference.

So by all means think carefully about what you want to do and why, but don't get attached to a specific outcome. The same game will work differently on a different day with a different group anyway. Which also makes life much more interesting for you.

Enough talk. Game on ...

Story of Your Name (pairs)

Tell your partner a story connected with your name.
Hear one from them. Swap partners. Tell a different one
to your new partner (or tell the same story differently).

Quickdraw (pairs)

Each person needs a pen. One shared sheet of paper.
Each person draws one line (or feature) at a time, quickly,
taking turns to create a face together. Once the face is
done, name the character by taking turns to write one
letter at a time underneath.

Presents (pairs)

First person mimes giving a present (don't decide what it is,
just define with a gesture). Receiver thanks them, unwraps
it, says what it is. Keep exchanging presents.

Extend this to make a story. Use the present for something,
do the obvious thing with it and see where it takes you.

Yes, and ... (group)

In a circle. Start with a sentence. Each person follows by
saying 'Yes, and...' adding to what came before to make
a story. Make sure people connect with the statement
that came just before them.

Character Circle (group)

In a circle. Each person says something about an imaginary
character they all know. Continues until the character is
fleshed out. You can follow the circle, or allow people to
add whenever they like.

First Letter, Last Letter (pairs/group)
Each speech in a scene or conversation has to start with a word that begins with the last letter of the last word spoken by the previous person. For example:

First person: *'What's next?'*
Second person: *'Time for something different, I think.'*

Word at a Time Expert/Story (group)
A team of five or six people become an expert and answers questions, or tell a story: one – word – at – a – time. Each person gets just one word and it passes on to the next person. The phrases should make grammatical sense, not be a list of words.

Djever (group)
The first person says *'Djever'* (a contraction of 'did you ever'). Then each player adds one word at a time to ask a question, e.g. *Djever. Ride. A. Pony. To. Zimbabwe?* When the sentence seems complete, they start a new inquiry by saying: *'Djever?'*

Swedish Story (pairs)
One storyteller, one word giver. A title from the rest of the group. The storyteller starts, and the other person throws in irrelevant words when they like (they can't throw in another word until the previous one has been used). Storyteller has to use the words.

Colour/Advance (pairs)
One person tells a story to a given title. The other asks them to colour (give more detail) or advance (move the action forward) as the story requires. They ask for whichever they want more of, as often as they like.

Five Words (pairs)
One person asks the other questions. They have to answer with only five words. Exactly. Not more, not less.

Unfinished Sentences (group)
Start telling a story (in a group) to a title. Each person leaves off wherever they want. The next person has to pick it up and continue exactly where the previous person left off.

Incorporations (group)
Self-organise into physical groups around questions or themes given by the facilitator (e.g. How long have you worked here? How are you feeling right now?). To work out who they are in a group with, they have to walk around and talk to lots of people.

Walk and Stop (group)
Everyone standing up, spread around the room. The rules are: if you see someone walking, you should walk. If you see someone stopped, you should stop. Anyone can choose to walk or choose to stop at any time.

One, Two, Three People Walking (group)
Everyone standing up spread around the room.
The facilitator states the number of people they want to be walking at a time. Anyone can stop or start whenever they like. The facilitator changes the number frequently.

How Many Reds? (group)
Ask people how many shades or spots of red they think there are in the room. Then ask them to look carefully and count.

One to Twenty (group)
Form a circle. Count through the numbers from one to twenty without creating a system or pattern. If two people say a number at the same time you go back to the beginning. If twenty is hard, try ten. If you get beyond twenty, see how far you can go.

Object Tap (group)
Choose an everyday object. List its qualities or attributes. Then pick qualities off that list and apply them to your problem, idea, issue or product. Ask: *'How could we make it smoother?'* Or: *'What would it mean for it to be round?'* Use this crashing together to spark off insights and ideas.

Shake Eight (group)
Standing. Shake right arm eight times, then left arm, right leg, left leg. Then seven times, six, five etc. Try to all follow the leader and stay coordinated.

Scavenger Hunts (group)
Facilitator gives people only a few seconds to go and find an object of a particular kind (e.g. one you hate, or love, or that is red, or that you don't know what it is, etc.). Make it a very short time — less than a minute. The hurry is part of it. Then talk about people's objects or use them for Object Tap, or to tell stories or share.

About the illustrations

The idea for the illustrations in this book were themselves an experiment in improvisation. Here is what Nick says about that process:

Working on these illustrations uncorked something in my artistic practice. Though I draw for my own pleasure, it's rare I do a project like this. When I do get a commission, I often get stuck on wanting to get it 'right' or 'good', and my drawing gets uptight.

I often doodle whilst I talk to people anyway, so one offer here was to do that whilst Rob talked about improvisation. I tried that for a bit and it was a good start, but it didn't quite click. I switched media, from pen and paper to an iPad and doodled while listening to the audiobook. During a description of one of the games, I realised 'this is a game too' with its own rules and constraints. That was what uncorked it.

What was really satisfying was discovering it worked best when I allowed myself to doodle until I got to the first 'juicy' image or idea (like 'what do they do with the feathers'). Then I'd settle on that, and finish it in one go. This combination of constraint and playfulness freed me up and enabled me to let go of the idea of 'getting it right'.

So yes, the drawings are the result of several little games and constraints, noticing and accepting and letting go.

Inviting Nick to do the illustrations lead to a new creative product for him. One wasn't the cause of the other, but, as he puts it, 'without this, not that'.

About the author

Robert Poynton divides his time between an off-grid, solar-powered house near Arenas de San Pedro (in rural Spain) and Oxford, where he is an Associate Fellow of the University's Saïd Business School.

For over twenty years he has been playing around with ideas from improv and how they can help outside the theatre. At Oxford, he uses the ideas described in this book to help leaders work with complex change.

Together with Gary Hirsh, he founded On Your Feet, a consultancy that uses these techniques and practices with companies and organisations. More recently he and Gary have created 'The Everyday Improviser' — a short online course designed to bring the benefits of these practices to anyone and everyone, easily and quickly.

Yellow, his current occupation, is another improvisational endeavour. It forms small online learning groups which are designed in response to the participants, not according to a pre-determined programme.

He has spoken and led workshops at the DO Lectures, The Skoll World Forum, Singularity University and Schumacher College. He is the author of *Do Pause: You are not a To Do list*, published by Do Books, 2019.

He is married with three sons. His wife runs an organic beef farm.

@robpoynton | robertpoynton.com

Thanks

First, thanks to Miranda at Do Books, who somehow manages to have a light touch and give clear direction at the same time, which is wonderful. Being invited to write by her, at the DO Lectures in 2011, was a turning point for me. The books themselves have brought me so many opportunities, connections and ideas that it is hard to imagine life without them.

Thanks to David Hieatt for creating the DO Lectures and to Andy Middleton for inviting me. Over ten years later, it still keeps giving.

To James Victore for a cover design that captures the spirit of what I am talking about perfectly. To Nick Parker, for the illustrations and for being willing to play around with how they were created.

Also to Eva Congil and Fernanda Ares at Koan Libros. The prospect of this edition being translated into Spanish was a great incentive for me. Gracias.

Thanks to Gary Hirsch at On Your Feet for being my improv point man over decades and such a joyful person to play with. To everyone else at On Your Feet for all the learning, input and fun over the years.

To Marshall Young and Tracey Camilleri at Oxford University for helping me see the bigger picture and giving me a platform to test these ideas with what seemed like an unlikely audience. Thanks also to all the people who have come to Oxford, for being bold enough to try this stuff and for giving me feedback and confidence as a result.

To Lisa Kay Solomon, Nick Parker (again!), Kirsten Gunnerud, Steve Chapman, Hugh Derrick and Johnnie Moore for sharing your experiences. To David Keating, for the illuminating conversations and insights into improv in the world of film. To Roland Harwood for constant inspiration through his podcast 'On The Edge'. To Leila Ferreira for the generous and kind offer of a place in Cascais to stay and write, just when I needed it. To Alex Carabi for accompanying me on the improvisational adventure that is Yellow. I could not wish for a wiser companion.

To my wife Beatriz for giving me practical support, encouragement and for listening to umpteen fragments read out loud. We all need to be heard, and that is particularly important for a writer.

This edition is dedicated to my three sons, Pablo, Mateo and Bruno, who will have to adapt and change far more than previous generations. Though they are oblivious, it is they who have taught me much of what I know about improvisation. I just hope that there is something here they might find useful one day.

Books in the series

Also available

Available in print, digital and audio formats from booksellers or via our website: **thedobook.co**

To hear about events, forthcoming titles and our book club, find us on social media **@dobookco**, or subscribe to our newsletter